STATEN ISLAND
SLAYINGS

STATEN ISLAND SLAYINGS

MURDERERS & MYSTERIES OF THE FORGOTTEN BOROUGH

PATRICIA M. SALMON

THE
History
PRESS

Published by The History Press
Charleston, SC 29403
www.historypress.net

Copyright © 2014 by Patricia M. Salmon
All rights reserved

First published 2014

Manufactured in the United States

ISBN 978.1.62619.755.8

Library of Congress CIP data applied for.

To Eleanore with all good wishes!

Peter [signature]

For Cheryl Criaris Bontales, a genuine Staten Island collector, historian and lifelong friend. We were fortunate to grow up in a neighborhood surrounded by history and historians.

CONTENTS

ACKNOWLEDGEMENTS

Sincere thanks to Barbara MacDonald Hemedinger, Megan Beck, Dawn Daniels, Michael Fressola, Fred DeLise, Friends of Abandoned Cemeteries of Staten Island, Ciro Galeno, Beth Gorrie, Dr. Thomas Matteo, the Noble Maritime Collection, Lynn Rogers, Staten Island OutLOUD and Erin Urban.

INTRODUCTION

Documentation of criminal activities of the past is certainly popular with the reading public. For this reason, a second volume focusing on Staten Island murders has been researched and presented with the hope that readers will continue to consider and contemplate the events of years gone by. Most importantly, it is hoped that these chronicles will enable all to remember the victims, especially those whose murders have never been solved. There are, unfortunately, many who fall within the boundaries of this category.

One killing that was documented and solved was preserved in not one, but two, Boston newspapers. While not surviving in any Staten Island newspapers, Kenneth Scott described it in a volume of *The Staten Island Historian* published by the Staten Island Historical Society in 1953. This horrific event took place in 1744, at a time when Staten Island was a rural enclave with farms spread sporadically across the island. Many individuals who received colonial land grants lived on properties comprising anywhere from several dozen to several thousand acres. Of course, the average farmer owned a more modest plot. These men were generally experts, or at least knowledgeable, on matters of naturally occurring flora, since they did not want their valuable farm animals nibbling on the toxic foliage that lined the borders of their agricultural property. In 1744, there was a Staten Island inhabitant who was learned in such matters. Married for only five months, he soon grew tired of his wife. As a matter of fact, he grew very tired of her. In late January or February of that year, this particularly weary fellow went afield to gather some herbs. Knowingly, he picked the most poisonous species he could locate. The devious collector brought the herbs home, handed them to his unsuspecting wife and told her to stuff a leg of veal with his fresh harvest.[1] Delighted to have such a fine addition to their evening repast, the wife gladly accepted the savory tidbits. Soon enough, the husband presented some reason to depart the premises and not partake of the repast with his wife, resulting in her consuming the veal dinner on her own. The woman fell ill. When he returned, the brutish husband demanded that she make him a meal, but not the veal. He did not want that; he wanted fried sausages. Even in her ailing condition, the good wife made his sausages, which he happily gobbled down with the result that he, too, became ill. He then asked his wife, "In what did you fry these sausages?" She responded, "In the gravy from the veal." To this, the husband replied, "I am a dead man." The two remained sick for some days with the result that they both expired. However, as the Boston newspapers quickly pointed out, the husband was first to die.[2]

NOTES TO THE READER

The county of Richmond was established by the English governor Thomas Dongan on November 1, 1683 . It was one of the original ten counties of what was then the province of New York. In 1788, Richmond was divided into the townships of Northfield, Westfield, Castleton and Southfield. In 1860, the new township of Middletown was carved out of portions of Castleton and Southfield. When the city of New York was consolidated in 1898, the resulting five boroughs included the official borough of Richmond. Prior to this occurrence, the island was generally referred to as the county of Richmond or Richmond County, with the old Dutch name of Staten Island sometimes used as well. In 1975, the official name was changed to Staten Island. Even so, Richmond and Staten Island are used interchangeably—officially and unofficially—with Staten Island being the more popular of the two unofficially.

The nineteenth and early twentieth centuries saw much confusion concerning streets on Staten Island, as many of their names were used multiple times on the island. In the early 1900s, a committee was formed to rectify this confusion. (One member of this committee was naturalist/ historian William T. Davis.) The work of these men resulted in many street name conversions in 1909. In 1915 and again around 1930, additional street names were amended. For this reason, there are streets documented in this book and others that no longer exist. Where possible, the current name has been included. It is also important for the reader to know that the Richmond Turnpike is now called Victory Boulevard. This name change occurred as a result of the victory realized at the close of World War I. In addition, the community we now refer to as Richmond Town was historically known simply as Richmond. Of major importance to readers and researchers is the fact that house and business address numbers were also altered. This process is said to have occurred around 1917.

Unfortunately, several of these chapters demonstrate the prejudice that is often unleashed on ethnic groups and women. They are distressing but true representations of the thought patterns of many individuals and groups—now and in the past. The prejudice and stereotyping relayed in some of these chapters is in no way representative of the author's beliefs or feelings and have been left intact, as they might have affected the event(s) described herein. They are important components of the accounts as they unfolded, and their removal would result in historical inaccuracy.

—

CHAPTER 1

FASCINATING DISCLOSURES

Reward—Mrs. Eliza Brannan has been missing from this city since last Tuesday afternoon at 3 o'clock (July 20) when she left Third Street on her way to the steamboat Thomas Hunt…*She was in appearance between 25 and 30 years of age, of medium size, light hair, blue eyes, low forehead, was dressed in mourning black hat and veil…*[3]

Mrs. Brannan had simply disappeared into the vapors of an unremarkable summer afternoon. No one knew where she was. If someone, anyone, could provide information leading to the establishment of her whereabouts, they would receive what was then a vast sum—$200. Two weeks later, the reward more than doubled to $500![4] To be compensated, the collector was advised to proceed to the office of Dr. Charles H. Crane at the U.S. Army Medical Purveyor's Office, 110 Grand Street, Manhattan. Dr. Crane was Mrs. Brannan's brother. Both were the offspring of Colonel Ichabod Crane. Indeed, the late Colonel Crane was a very real person. When Washington Irving met Ichabod Crane at Sackett's Harbor, New York, in 1814, he was fascinated with the man's name and determined to use it in his literary endeavors, hence the famous character in the famous short story "The Legend of Sleepy Hollow." It is important to note that the schoolteacher and the real Ichabod Crane have absolutely nothing in common other than their name.

Born in Elizabeth, New Jersey, on July 18, 1787, the real Ichabod Crane was a graduate of West Point. Eventually, he climbed through army ranks and

Colonel Ichabod Crane, father of Eliza Crane Brannan, circa 1850. *Library of Congress.*

was appointed a colonel in the First United States Artillery. After the close of the Mexican-American War, sometime around 1850, Crane purchased a farm on the Richmond Turnpike (now Victory Boulevard) near Signs Road in the Chelsea Heights section of Staten Island. Akin to a social headquarters for visiting army officers, Crane did not enjoy this new homestead for long, as he passed into the next life on October 5, 1857. The colonel was buried with strict military honors at the Springville Cemetery, now part of the Asbury Methodist Episcopal Cemetery on Richmond Avenue in New Springville. (A unique obelisk monument to his memory is visible at the burial ground today.) General Winfield Scott was just one of the many esteemed members of the armed forces present at his burial.

Ichabod and Charlotte Crane had three children. The previously mentioned Dr. Charles Crane would rise to the rank of U.S surgeon general. Another son, William, was well known on Staten Island and would eventually be buried at New Springville, too. Their daughter, Eliza Crane Brannan, is the subject of this narrative.

Eliza Crane married career military man John Brannan on September 16, 1850. At this time, Brannan was a captain. While Brannan was stationed in Key West, Florida, Eliza contracted a serious fever. Fortunately, she did recover, but it was said that the illness left her with recurrent headaches, and she often took to her bed. On the advice of her physician brother, Eliza and her daughter, Alida, left Key West and returned to Staten Island, where they lived with Mrs. Charlotte Crane in the family home on the Richmond Turnpike.

When Eliza Brannan vanished, conflicting reports on her whereabouts began to arrive. One announcement declared that she was last seen in Manhattan; however, this proved untrue, as reliable witnesses eventually revealed that she had made her way to Staten Island, where she was observed getting into a carriage at the Quarantine ferry landing (vicinity of today's Bay Street Landing) with a man dressed entirely in black. It was immediately believed by all that she met with a violent death, "for to suppose that she is voluntarily absent is forbidden by every circumstance of her life by her devotion as a wife and mother, her only child having been left at her mother's on Staten Island. She may have been abducted, she may have been drowned, but, viewed in any light the disappearance at such a time is very mysterious."[5] Police were said to be "very chary" in providing details, since they feared publicity would defeat their cause. Carriage drivers at the Quarantine ferry dock were collected and interrogated. One individual's responses were so confused that he was immediately arrested. It was expected and loudly announced that his interview by the authorities would provide interesting revelations. Many voiced the belief that additional arrests were imminent. Police soon became desperate and sent an officer to both Boston and Nantucket, where Mrs. Brannan had

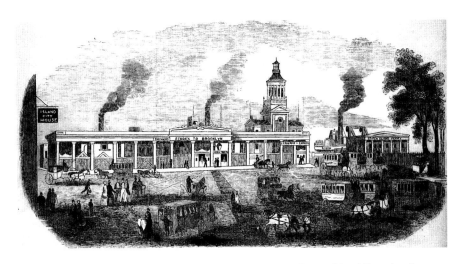

Initially, Eliza Brannan was believed to have vanished at the Staten Island Ferry landing at Whitehall, Manhattan, on July 20, 1858. *From* Gleason's Pictorial, *1853.*

previously resided. The expedition revealed nothing. The newspapers wanted answers (and readers). One daily penned: "Who is safe" if one's wife or sister could be "spirited away, in broad daylight, by any of the thousand or more hackmen" residents used daily?[6] It was finally realized that the incarcerated driver was innocent, so he was eventually released. All were mystified. Rumors swirled that Mrs. Brannan was accosted by a man while on the ferryboat as it passed through the harbor. Still others were fixated on the man in black who had entered the carriage with Mrs. Brannan. Police searched the woods, dales, swamps and ponds along her supposed route between the Quarantine and Port Richmond, as they had reached the conclusion that Mrs. Brannan had been violated, murdered and deposited in a roadside ditch or body of water. One detective reportedly located Eliza Brannan at West Point, New York, but instead of telegraphing her description to headquarters, he returned to the city for proof of her identity. When he returned to West Point, the description in hand was useless, as the woman had disappeared.

On September 21, Captain John Brannan arrived in New York City to commence his own investigation. It had taken the captain quite some time to procure leave from his Florida post. Brannan brought in former chief of police George W. Matsell, Esq., to find his wife, with the result that Matsell had all the wetlands along Mrs. Brannan's route dragged. However, no body or remains were found. With no new leads, Brannan had all involved individuals re-interrogated. Mrs. Eliza Crane Brannan was not located or any new information uncovered.

"A lady of refined education and demeanor...religious in feeling, fond of literature, of a domestic disposition, affectionate and devoted as daughter, mother, sister, and wife" was how one newspaper described Mrs. Brannan.[7] Owing to her "relations with family and society," no one believed she would "withhold the fact that she was alive" and cause such extended worry.[8] Eliza had, in fact, planned a visit to Maine and New Hampshire with a friend, and she was said to be looking forward to the trip. Captain Brannan had also received correspondence from his wife that she would be returning to Key West in the fall and had already bought and shipped new furniture to this location. When she vanished on that July day, Eliza had a parasol and was wearing her wedding ring, a diamond ring, a watch and chain and the clothing she had selected that morning. With only a small amount of money in her possession, everything she owned was in the family home at Chelsea Heights. For these reasons, most feared that she was murdered the night of July 20, 1858, but there were some who believed otherwise.

By early 1859, discussion of Mrs. Brannan's whereabouts had subsided, although one report had surfaced in August 1858 stating that she had been observed at both the Glen House and the Tip Top House in New Hampshire's Presidential Range. By February 1859, friends of Eliza Brannan were offering a $1,000 reward for information leading to her discovery—dead or alive. An outlandish account did arrive in April of that year. Supposedly, Mrs. Brannan's remains were found in a soapbox at the Hudson River railroad depot in Albany, New York. Upon examination, this declaration was completely refuted. The body in the box was actually "an old lady who had been dead for several years and had doubtless been packed and shipped for cheap transportation as a medical subject."[9] About sixty or seventy years old, the corpse had only two teeth, one on either side of the lower jaw about two inches apart. The rest of her teeth had been removed fifteen to twenty years earlier. In no way did this resemble Eliza Brannan. But such are the reports received by authorities when individuals disappear mysteriously.

All were shocked in March 1860, when the *New York Tribune* heralded that Mrs. Brannan was in the bloom of health and living in Italy. The Crane family vehemently refuted this report and declared that they would hold the newspaper responsible for what they felt was an irresponsible, misleading story. On March 20, an obscure newspaper from Ellicottville, New York, the *American Union*, reported that a private letter was received from an unknown entity stating that it was true, Mrs. Brannan was living

Ichabod Crane, John Brannan and Powell T. Wyman were all graduates of the West Point Military Academy in New York. Original painting by William Wall, circa 1821. *Library of Congress.*

Opposite: Brigadier General John M. Brannan during the Civil War, circa 1862. *Library of Congress.*

and breathing in Florence, Italy. Sighted and recognized by persons who knew her well, Mrs. Brannan was not alone. Mrs. Brannan, with the emphasis on Mrs., had eloped with First Lieutenant Powell T. Wyman of the First Regiment. The lieutenant had been under the command of Captain John Brannan. An 1851 graduate of West Point, Wyman was a native of Massachusetts. Most importantly, Wyman and Eliza had fallen in love.

When the acquaintance neared Eliza in Florence, she shouted out the missing woman's name, after which Eliza took on a "death-like paleness" and was rendered speechless.[10] At this time, she was in the company of Wyman. The two were subsequently seen together on several occasions. Research soon revealed that Wyman's passport covered both he and his "wife."[11] Further disclosure alleged that Wyman had, in fact, had trouble with his superior officer, Captain John Brannan. Actually, it was Brannan who had "trouble" with Wyman, as Wyman was discovered "touching"

his wife while all three were at the Key West military base.[12] Wyman left thereafter on a leave of absence.

When the Civil War began in 1861, Wyman returned to the U.S. Army on the Union side. As colonel of the Sixteenth Massachusetts Regiment, Wyman was the officer in charge. The colonel and his men passed through New York City on August 18, 1861, on their way to a Jersey City steamer that was readying for departure to Washington. More than one person criticized Massachusetts governor John Andrew for appointing an adulterer to such a high commission.

By March 1862, Captain Brannan was Brigadier General John Brannan. More importantly, he was done with his wife, having filed for divorce on the grounds of adultery in the District of Columbia Circuit Court.

Colonel Powell Wyman, the man who had profoundly changed the life of Eliza Crane Brannan, took a bullet through the heart at the Battle of Glendale, Virginia, on June 30, 1862. Wyman succumbed to the battlefield

Statue of Governor John Andrew, who appointed Colonel Powell Wyman commander of the Sixteenth Massachusetts Regiment, circa 1903. *Library of Congress*.

shooting and died. An account of the events of his death states that his orderly, Waldo Olaflin, and others carried the body of their slain colonel eight miles and buried him under a tree. Since they were in enemy territory, it was clearly marked with the hope that it would be reclaimed when peace returned. It was further stated that Olaflin removed a miniature of Eliza from Wyman's bosom. When it was returned to Eliza, she became inconsolable. Wyman's dead body was retrieved and shipped back to Eliza sooner than expected, and the thirty-four-year-old soldier was laid in state at the Massachusetts State House in Boston on July 22. A corps of cadets stood solemnly at guard, while flags throughout Boston were flown at half-mast. Upon leaving the state house, Wyman's remains were escorted by the Second Regiment State Militia, Governor John A. Andrew and his staff, several Masonic lodges, numerous military officers and members of the city government to Mount Auburn Cemetery in Cambridge, Massachusetts, for interment.

The Supreme Court of the District of Columbia granted a decree of absolute divorce in favor of General John Brannan against his wife, Eliza, in the spring of 1863. In addition, the court gave the general custody of their only child. Chief Justice Carter wrote, "That the wife, in 1858, in one of those strange and wicked caprices that sets at defiance the vows of marriage, and the obligations of honor, of respectable parentage and respectable kindred, broke loose from her marriage relations and took up her abode with a Mr. Powell T. Wyman…[She took his name] and returned to this country under his title—braving public opinion, and withal disregarding the moral sense of propriety of society," all of which resulted in great agony and anxiety for the general.[13] Carter continued by noting that Brannan was unsure whether she had committed suicide or was wandering about in a demented state and "that he expended his time and money in raking the lakes and advertising in the highways to ascertain her whereabouts…All of this time it appears she was cruelly speculating in prostitution," even though she knew her husband was desperate to find her.[14] The fact that she refused to acknowledge that she was alive and well for a full two years was, according to Carter, one of the cruelest instances of infidelity on record.

On the occasion of this divorce, the *Daily National Republican* of May 22, 1863, published its version of the affair between Wyman and Mrs. Brannan, entitled "The Brannan Divorce Case: A Romantic Story." The newspaper stated that Mrs. Brannan was so alienated from John Brannan that she decided to leave him. Moving to Italy, she and Wyman developed a correspondence through a mutual friend, although the two knew each other nominally. Mention was made that Wyman was under the command of John Brannan at some point during his military career. Through the correspondence, the two became enamored of each other, and Wyman applied for a leave of absence from his military career to visit Eliza in Italy. The request was refused. Thus, he resigned his commission and departed for Europe. The two married. Wyman wrote to Brannan, informing him that if "he desired any satisfaction for the injury," he would provide it.[15] Supposedly, Brannan went to Europe to meet with Wyman, but no violence came of the encounter. Soon afterward, Wyman and Eliza Brannan returned to America and made their home in Boston. When the Sixteenth Regiment was organized, Wyman was placed in command. It was said he had an excellent reputation as a military officer.

Suffering from chronic dyspepsia, General John M. Brannan died suddenly on December 16, 1892. By 1875, he had taken a second wife, but his obituary did not mention her or her name. Only his married daughter by Eliza was indicated, and only as Mrs. A.B. Talbot. It was noted that Brannan had graduated from West Point in 1841. He saw service in the Mexican War commencing in 1842 and also during battles with the Seminole Indians in Florida. As a brigadier general during the Civil War, he was involved with numerous battles and campaigns. In 1865, he became a major general. Brannan retired from military service on April 19, 1882.

According to the Mount Auburn Cemetery website, Eliza Crane Brannan Wyman's date of death and burial are both October 26, 1892. She is not interred with Colonel Powell T. Wyman but rather a short walk away from the grave site of her beloved.

CHAPTER 2

THE REFUSAL

Supposedly, he loved her, but her death implied otherwise. Perhaps he loved her, but it was on his own terms, in his own way—his own obsessed, irrational way.

On Wednesday, September 6, 1848, Mary Slaight was left to die at the Manhattan address where she had sought safety from an insane husband and a brutal marriage. For twenty years, Mary had been married to John Slaight. They had six children together. When she fled their Rossville, Staten Island residence for a secure refuge in Manhattan, the thirty-five-year-old wife and mother took her three youngest children to a basement apartment at 161 Hammond Street (now West Eleventh Street). Two of their offspring remained at Rossville, and another daughter was protected, as she worked and lived as a domestic elsewhere. Before Mary fled to Manhattan, John Slaight had attempted to kill her on at least three occasions: once with a knife, once with a gun and once with an axe. Crafty but inefficient, John Slaight was a mentally unbalanced alcoholic who could not provide for himself, much less his family. After Mary's escape, Slaight sought her out on several occasions in an attempt to lure her home. But Mary was a wise woman and refused each request, stating that she did not trust his "future conduct."[16] A desperate Slaight made one final attempt at 5:00 p.m. on September 6, 1848. When he asked Mary if she still persisted in her refusal to live with him, she replied that she would have moved back with him at one point, "but that time was gone."[17] Realizing her resolve, Slaight insisted on the final word. Removing a pistol from his pocket, he pointed it at Mary. Brave woman that she was, Mary sprang forward to grab the gun, but she was not quick enough. Slaight emptied the contents of the gun into her neck and fled. The entire tragedy was viewed by their young daughter, whose hysterical screams brought upstairs neighbors to the scene. Dr. James P. Steward arrived and did all that could be done to save Mary, but she died three days later. The postmortem revealed that one of the shots had gone "through the soft parts of the neck to the sixth vertebrae, the ball having passed through the vertebrae" and divided the "spinal marrow."[18]

John Slaight's escape brought him to Blazing Star, New Jersey, where he attempted to secret himself along the Arthur Kill River farm of a Mr. Abrahams. Discovered, the murderer was brought in a weakened condition to Abrahams's farmhouse, where the kind owner attempted to aid his exhausted "visitor." Abrahams had no idea he was assisting a killer. Interestingly, Blazing Star was opposite Rossville, Staten Island, which had also historically been called Blazing Star, after a tavern of that same name. Historically, a ferry crossed the Arthur Kill between the two villages. Fortunately, the owner of the Blazing Star Hotel, a Mr. Tuft, recognized Slaight, who was immediately removed to Rossville by boat and handed over to Richmond County sherriff Guion (Guyon). Slaight responded by trying to slit his own throat in a suicide attempt, but the act was prevented by his custodian. Sherriff Guion persuaded Slaight to admit that he had bought a gun at a Manhattan store and then proceeded to Hammond Street, where he gave his wife the ultimatum. Slaight claimed that he had no intention of slaying her. (Did he think threatening her life with the weapon would induce her to return home?) Exhausted and insane, Slaight still understood that his actions and their consequences were serious. Removed to the City Prison in Manhattan, Slaight's weakened condition was exacerbated by diarrhea, refusal to take sustenance and blood loss from the suicide attempt. On the afternoon of September 12, Slaight finally drank some milk punch (a concoction of milk, sugar, vanilla and, not surprisingly, bourbon). After ingestion, the murderer died. Conscious to the end, he requested "that he might be permitted to die quietly, being fully aware as he expressed himself, that there was no hope for him to escape an ignominious death on the gallows."[19] Two prison employees were assigned to "attend him" with instructions that they "render him as comfortable as circumstances would admit," which was quite generous, as it was more than he allowed for Mary.[20] Sensible until death arrived, Slaight never professed any sorrow for Mary's murder. Since he was a Staten Island native, the slayer was removed from the City Prison and handed over to his relations for interment. The forty-five-year-old's demise was listed as suicide by starvation.

CHAPTER 3

KILLED BY
A SWORD CANE

Laborer James Field was on an isolated path taking a mealtime walk through the Green estate between Castleton and Brighton Avenues in New Brighton when, much to his surprise, he found a lifeless body. Field was a worker at the Louis Dejonge Paper Company on the Richmond Turnpike near Silver Lake, a plant that specialized in the manufacture of fancy papers. It was Saturday, April 5, 1884. Instead of saving a few precious minutes for his noontime meal, Field was waylaid by his discovery of a man who had been stabbed in the chest. Subsequent examination revealed another gash, this one on the back shoulder. Across the right shoulder of the deceased was the blade of a sword cane—a cane created with a hollow shaft to secret a sheath or a sword. Here was something else peculiar: the dead man's wounds were not made by the mysterious sword cane positioned across his torso. They came from another blade.

The coroner was summoned. He arrived soon enough to realize that the body was still warm and that the man's gold pocket watch was still running (watches needed to be wound in 1884). A twenty-dollar gold piece was on his person, as were thirteen dollar bills (not a lucky number for the recently departed). Since the scabbard had gone right through the victim's body, the coroner had no doubt it was murder and not suicide. A heavy, gold seal ring with the letters "F" and "M" cut into onyx was observed on the third finger of the left hand, while his shirt sleeves bore gold cuff buttons with the letter "F." It was noted that the corpse was well dressed and had brown hair, a mustache and an imperial (a small, pointed beard beneath the lip). Other

Louis DeJonge & Co.,

Importers and Manufacturers of

FANCY PAPERS

MOROCCOS,

Russia and Other Leather,

ENGLISH BOOK CLOTH,

CHROMOS,

PICTURES, PAPER LACES,

BORDERS,

SCRAP ✦ BOOK ✦ PICTURES.

FACTORY ON STATEN ISLAND.

Office and Warerooms: 71 & 73 Duane Street,

NEW YORK.

Employed by Louis De Jonge and Company, James Field was on a meal break when he found Carmilio Farach. *From* An Illustrated Sketch Book of Staten Island, *1886.*

than the initials on the buttons and the rings, there was nothing to identify this well-groomed male. It did not take long, though. It was soon determined that the man lying dead on the New Brighton path was Carmilio Farach. Approximately forty-five years old, he was a Brooklyn cigar dealer.

Before Carmilio's remains were identified in Staten Island, his brother Ramondo had become concerned about his missing sibling. Ramondo soon discovered that Carmilio was last seen in the company of Antonio Flaccomio as the two headed for the Staten Island Ferry terminal at Whitehall. When questioned by Ramondo, Flaccomio went "pale" and "replied gruffly: 'Your brother was in New-York [Manhattan] yesterday and had trouble with a man.'"[21] Ramondo asked, "Who was the man?" to which Flaccomio responded, "I don't know, but a barber in South-street—Lanzirotti—saw him and will tell you."[22] Ramondo then requested that Flaccomio show him the barbershop. After numerous excuses about why he could not accompany him, Flaccomio relented and brought Ramondo to Lanzirotti's business. When they arrived, Flaccomio refused to enter and stood on the curb while Ramondo spoke with the barber. It was then that Lanzirotti informed Ramondo that his brother was dead. He then handed Ramondo a newspaper documenting Field's discovery of the body on Staten Island. Lanzirotti said he knew nothing about the murder, but he told Ramondo to press Flaccomio for details. The barber pointed out that the two were together the day before and that when Flaccomio returned to the barbershop afterward, his appearance was much altered. Not only was he attired in a completely different suit of clothes, but Flaccomio now had a black eye and was badly bruised. In response to questioning, Flaccomio claimed the bruises were from neuralgia that had set in since that morning.

Ramondo Farach left for Staten Island to view the body, now held at the morgue. It was Carmilio. Ramondo informed the police that the sword cane found on the body belonged to his brother. Near hysterics from scrutinizing his murdered brother's corpse, Ramondo lamented, "See where he tried to defend himself from the stiletto, and see where he fell on his knees when struck down…"[23] The knees of Carmilio's trousers were filthy with mud.

Ramondo told the authorities that Carmilio, Antonio and a woman named Filippa Teresa had opened a Brooklyn cigar store at 103 Degraw Street. According to Ramondo, the business was plagued by financial difficulties, with Flaccomio consistently indebted to Carmilio. This resulted in bitter and often violent arguments between the two men. During this

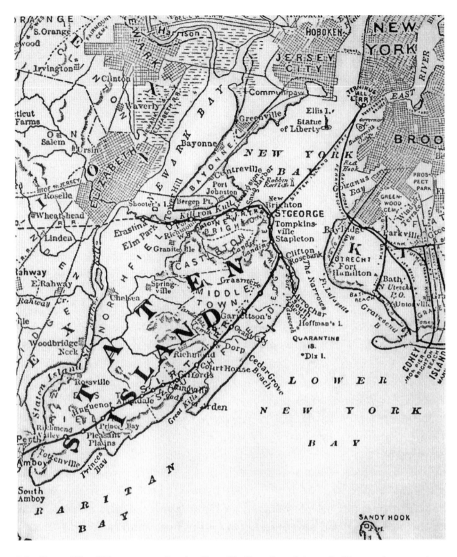

The Staten Island Ferry route taken by Carmilio Farach and Antonio Flaccomio to reach the dueling ground. *From* Rides and Rambles on Staten Island, *1889.*

time, Flaccomio married Teresa, who was also now dead. Ramondo Farach then went before Judge Kullman of Stapleton and charged that Antonio Flaccomio had information about the murder of his sibling. A warrant was issued and Flaccomio arrested. Police described Flaccomio as "being an exceedingly handsome man, 40 years of age, and wonderfully built. When he was captured Flaccomio was frightened to death" and so nervous that police thought he would confess to the murder before the night was over "if, as the Sergeant on duty wryly stated…he is properly worked."[24]

Rumors circulated that the murder occurred over spousal jealousy, while others contended it was over the sale of goods that brought a large profit to Carmilio. Much was made in the media of the fact that the men were Sicilian and that the scores of such individuals were settled by duels. As was common at this time and for many decades to come, prejudice against Italians and other immigrants was rampant in the media.

On April 12, 1884, Antonio Flaccomio was released for lack of evidence, with Carmilio's death listed as a suicide. It was noted that Flaccomio now had a severe case of erysipelas, an acute streptococcal infectious disease of the skin that was accompanied by fever, headache, vomiting and purplish raised lesions on his face. Flaccomio might have been a fine-looking man, but he was not a healthy specimen. He also disappeared at this time, with no one able to determine whether he was dead or alive.

This odd story took an odder turn two years later, when a man named Antonio Ferconio appeared in Brooklyn during the third week of July 1886. It was actually Antonio Flaccomio assuming another identity. Flaccomio had quietly slipped back into Brooklyn and asked for a meeting with Ramondo Farach. The purpose was to clear his guilty conscience. Flaccomio believed that Carmilio was "killed in a perfectly fair encounter," but of his homecoming and subsequent confession, Flaccomio bemoaned that "night after night, where ever he went he was haunted by the apparition of Carmilio" and that "ill luck had followed him" everywhere.[25] He realized that to find relief, he must profess to Ramondo what occurred on Staten Island that day. Carmilio Farach had died by Flaccomio's hand. The latter admitted to Ramondo that an awful quarrel had occurred between the two. Both believed the only way to settle the matter honorably was by a duel. Their weapons of choice were sword canes. Carmilio fell during the fight and landed on his sword, taking a mortal wound. Flaccomio was "penitent on making his confession and wanted to kiss" Ramondo.[26] Instead, Ramondo shook his hand, as he believed his brother was killed in an "affair of honor." Ramondo promised Flaccomio he would not inform the authorities, but he told Flaccomio to leave Brooklyn and never return. Ramondo warned him: "If you return, I will kill you."[27] Of course, Flaccomio denied that he took the $400 that was said to have been in Carmilio's pocket the day he died. During his two-year absence, Flaccomio had visited Louisiana,

Buffalo, Louisville and Chicago—considerable travel for someone with serious financial problems.

The mysterious Flaccomio, who, over the years, was a gambler, counterfeiter and even a count, came to a vicious end. On October 14, 1888, he was knifed to death on a curb outside Cooper Union in Manhattan. The murder weapon was specifically placed next to his body. While he lay dead on the ground, it was observed that "he looked to be an Italian of good circumstance."[28] In fact, he was doing well in the grocery business at this time. Police theorized that Ramondo Farach orchestrated the stabbing to avenge Carmilio's demise four years earlier.

On the evening of his death, Flaccomio had a festive time eating, drinking and playing an Italian finger game known as "tocco" in La Trinacria on Saint Mark's Place in Manhattan. The knife found next to Flaccomio's lifeless body was traced to the restaurant. Six individuals were with Flaccomio that night, and police reported that considerable amounts of Chianti and liquor had been consumed. Three of the six men were arrested. Authorities were unable to find the other three, owing to the reticence of the Italian community in speaking to law enforcement.

A local newspaperman went to Ramondo Farach's photography shop for an interview. The reporter unabashedly wrote, "Although he speaks English with the peculiarities of the Italian, he is gentle and almost refined."[29] When informed that he was suspected in the murder, Farach's eyes twinkled. When asked why he did not prosecute Flaccomio for killing his brother, Ramondo said he did not want Flaccomio hanged for murder. It seems that another Farach brother was married to a Flaccomio sister in Italy, and the death of Flaccomio would make this woman feel bad.

On October 22, 1888, the *Evening World* headline blared: "It Is the Mafia Now." Flaccomio was believed to be the victim of a "powerful, secret Sicilian society."[30] Accused as a member, police said Flaccomio spilled organizational secrets and was murdered by brothers Carlo and Vincenzo Quartararo, who were fruit men by day. When confronted by a reporter about the murder, Vincenzo laughed heartily and stated he was nowhere near the murder scene that evening. Carlo took off for Italy. Vincenzo was prosecuted for the murder but released after the jury disagreed about his conviction. The demise of Carmilio Farach was resolved, but to this day, the murder of Antonio Flaccomio remains cloaked in mystery.

CHAPTER 4

"YOU'LL EXPOSE ME; I KNOW YOU WILL!"

Sailors' Snug Harbor was generally a pleasant, tranquil locale on the Shore Road in Livingston, Staten Island. (It is now the Snug Harbor Cultural Center on Richmond Terrace.) Opened on August 1, 1833, "The Harbor" began operating as a refuge for "aged, decrepit and worn-out sailors" who had nowhere to go when they were no longer physically, or perhaps mentally, able to work. The endowment for the establishment and care of these seamen was provided by Robert Richard Randall, who inherited a substantial sum of money from his father—a man who made his fortune from maritime activities. This was one of the first retirement homes in the United States. Everything needed to sustain a large group of men was eventually established on the property, including dormitories, kitchens, dining halls, a farm and, of course, a chapel. Once the men arrived, their needs were filled; nutrition, shelter, recreation, religion and medical care were all provided. If able bodied, the men were required to assist with maintaining the grounds or the farm. Relaxation took the form of games such as dominoes, basket making, reading or simply watching the boats sail calmly along the Kill Van Kull.[31]

The trustees of this institution believed that providing religious guidance was one of their prime responsibilities. Since its earliest days, residents of Sailors' Snug Harbor were expected to attend all religious services unless prevented by illness or some extraordinary occurrence. Prayer sessions were held twice daily, once in the morning and once in the evening. Of paramount importance was Sunday service, which was, of course, mandatory. Worship

Partial view of the magnificent front five Greek Revival structures at Sailors' Snug Harbor. *From* Century Magazine, *Volume 28, June 1884.*

"Inmates" occupied in the workshop of Sailors' Snug Harbor. *From* Century Magazine, *Volume 28, June 1884.*

was presented along the creeds of either the Episcopal or Presbyterian faiths. In 1848, the trustees appointed a full-time chaplain to the institution. Initially, services were conducted in the central building (now Building C) facing the Kill Van Kull. Construction began on a permanent chapel for the men in 1854. The official opening took place during the autumn of 1856. At this initial assemblage, a Reverend Phillips warned the sailors that they were at the harbor to "refit" and must realize that the remainder of their lives would be filled with "quicksands, concealed rocks, whirlpools, and yawning gulphs."[32] They must be vigilant as "a darker, severer, and more terrific storm, and a more awful warring of the elements" might await them, with the result that they could "yet be hopelessly wrecked and left to sink."[33] These were sharp, stirring words that warned of the years ahead. By this time, there were three hundred souls listening—or maybe not.

Robert Quinn was born in 1798. His first career was that of a sailor. A change of heart guided him to the New Brunswick Seminary, where he became licensed to preach in 1833. It is not known when he began providing religious guidance at Sailors' Snug Harbor, but on the morning of January 31, 1863, Reverend Quinn led prayers for the "inmates," as residents of such institutions were then called. After the service, Reverend Quinn was departing the chapel (which still stands today and is known as the Veteran's Memorial Hall) when he encountered resident Herman Engle, who would later be referred to as both Herman Ingalls and Herman Engles. Deemed to be harmlessly insane (if there is such a thing), Mr. Engle bellowed at Quinn, "You'll expose me; I know you will, if you live."[34] Not wanting to take any chances on such an exposure, real or imagined, Engle withdrew a double-barreled gun from his breast pocket and fired into Reverend Quinn. The shot hit the minister below his heart. Quinn cried out, as best he could, "I'm shot. I'm shot." Reeling for several seconds, he fell dead to the ground. No sooner had the homicide been completed than Engle put the barrel of the gun next to his head. Releasing a second bullet, he sent his lower jaw across the lawn. Engle was dead within the hour.

Sometime during his time at "The Harbor," the reverend had reprimanded Herman Engle for some offense that no one knew of or recalled. But Engle obviously had a long memory and ruminated on the supposed scolding. In addition to wanting retribution, he needed to be satisfied that no one else would discover his offense. As a matter of fact, Engle had previously approached Quinn about the episode. He pleaded with the reverend to not "expose" him, with Quinn replying to not bother him with the matter. Quinn did mention the conversation to his wife. Some believed Engle had

Chapel, Sailors' Snug Harbor, where Herman Engle shot and killed Reverend Robert Quinn. *From* An Illustrated Sketch Book of Staten Island, *1886.*

Opposite, top: Ineligible for burial in the Sailors' Snug Harbor Cemetery, murderer Herman Engle was interred north of the cemetery fence. *From* An Illustrated Sketch Book of Staten Island, *1886.*

Opposite, bottom: "Inmates" relaxing outdoors at Sailors' Snug Harbor years after the murder, circa 1912. *Library of Congress.*

confided a past crime, perhaps even a murder, to the reverend. Having attempted to lift the burden from his mind, Engle was instead plagued by thoughts of Quinn publicly revealing his misdeed(s), with the result that Engle committed murder to conceal his secret.

Engle had been acting strangely on the morning of the shooting. Early on, he stationed himself at the corner of the chapel. A resident of Sailors' Snug Harbor for approximately seventeen years, Engle was a native of Norway. At the time of this horrific shooting, he was seventy-seven years old. It was never determined whether Engle had really done anything worthy of consuming him with such fear.

The funeral for Reverend Quinn took place at Sailors' Snug Harbor. Every inmate of the institution was present and accounted for in the same chapel that Quinn was exiting when he was slain by Engle. During the service, his body was placed in front of the pulpit from which he once preached. Afterward, the Reverend Robert Quinn was removed from Staten Island and buried at Hyde Park, New York.

Inmate Engle was not given a traditional burial at either of the Sailors' Snug Harbor cemeteries on the south side of the institution's grounds. Instead, he was buried north of the graveyard fence in what was then an anonymous field. "The only person officiating at his service" was the gravedigger.[35] No graveside prayer from the clergy was provided for the harmlessly insane retired seaman.

CHAPTER 5

A KNIFE IN THE TEMPLE

Edward Drurer was a rough character. Even so, the sketchy twenty-six-year-old was employed at the Standard Oil Works in Bayonne, New Jersey. On Saturday evening, October 10, 1885, Drurer was looking for a good time, and if he had to harass someone to instigate it, well, that was OK with him. It was a shame, too, because before the night ended, so would his life.

Work on the north shore line of the Staten Island Rapid Transit was progressing nicely. It was part of Erastus Wiman's transportation overhaul of Staten Island. St. George would be the final terminus point to reach Manhattan by ferryboat. It would be fed by east, north and south shore rail lines. The north shore line would eventually head west to a rail bridge at Old Place (not far from present-day Goethals Bridge), where goods would be transported to New Jersey and beyond. While under construction, the north shore line employed many men. On this night, with their pay in their pockets, Ferrand Barbour and John Hutchinson visited Charles Rappenhagen's North Shore House near the Kill Van Kull shoreline in West New Brighton for a few well-earned drinks. As surveyors, they spent their days steadily working to ready the rail line for service. They heard that a festive party was planned that evening to celebrate the opening of a new billiard hall at Rappenhagen's. In addition, revelers would be treated to a display of skill by billiard experts. By all accounts, Hutchinson and Barbour were enjoying themselves that evening. "After watching the playing for a while the two young men began to call for mixed drinks until they were in a hilarious state of intoxication."[36] Drurer, who was unknown to the two surveyors, was asked to join their fun. When Barbour bought him a drink, Drurer observed the considerable amount of money Barbour held since his pay consisted of several months' wages. Onlookers soon noticed that Drurer was purposely looking for a quarrel with Barbour. He "jostled" Barbour and threatened, "I can whip any dude that sports a high hat and a short coat."[37] (Barbour's hat was made of silk, while Hutchinson wore a contemporary bicycling outfit.) Rappenhagen intervened. He told Drurer that Hutchinson and Barbour were his guests and that he would "not have them interfered with." Drurer replied, "All right, Rapp. I'll stop."[38] It did not last. Drurer again antagonized the two men, eventually striking one of the surveyors in the face and tossing Barbour down a flight of stairs. Drurer and eight of his hooligan friends were then ejected from the tavern. Unfortunately, Barbour and Hutchinson decided to leave shortly thereafter. As they headed out, Drurer and his ruffian pals were waiting. Fearing for their pay and their safety, Barbour and Hutchinson ran. They made it fifty yards past the Young Men's Christian Association near present-day Tompkins Court on the Shore Road (now Richmond Terrace) but were overtaken by Drurer, who began pummeling one of them. Barbour responded by drawing a six-inch knife, which he thrust into Drurer's left temple. The knife was later found buried up to its hilt in Drurer's head! Taken to the S.R. Smith Infirmary, Drurer died three days later. Outside the courthouse, Barbour admitted, "It was I that struck the blow with the knife in self-defence [sic]."[39]

The residents of Staten Island turned out in force for the proceedings against Hutchinson and Barbour. Justice William J. Powers called for the release of Hutchinson, but Barbour was retained for prosecution on a felonious assault charge. Local newspapers plainly stated it would be a "celebrated" case.

On October 22, 1885, Ferrand Barbour was sentenced to eighteen months at Sing Sing Prison for manslaughter in the second degree. Because it was obvious self-defense, the public was greatly surprised and indignant with this outcome. Many called for an immediate pardon.

On November 5, 1885, Barbour was moved from the Richmond County Jail by Sherriff Brown and quietly escorted to the notorious Sing Sing Prison in Ossining, New York. Fearing for the prisoner's safety, or perhaps their own safety, law enforcement removed Barbour under great secrecy.

Erastus Wiman would have none of it, however, and he called for Barbour's immediate release. In response to Wiman's plea, the well-respected Reverend Dr. John C. Eccleston, rector of Saint John's Church

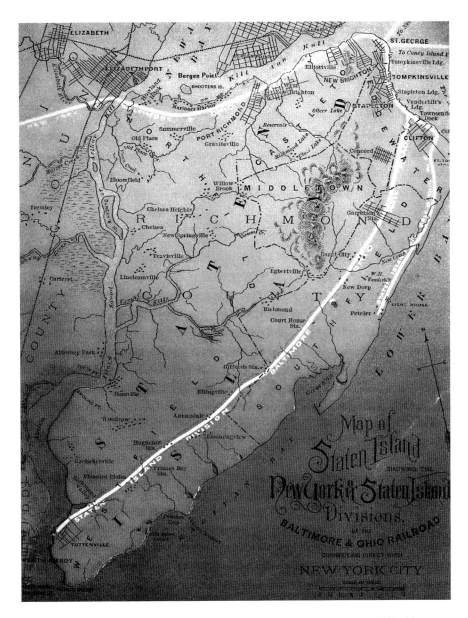

A map showing Wiman's overall transportation plan. Surveyors Barbour and Hutchinson were working on the northern portion of the project. *From* Toasts and Responses, *1885*.

This proposed rail bridge over the Arthur Kill River was to connect the north shore railroad with New Jersey. *From* An Illustrated Sketch Book of Staten Island, *1886.*

The Staten Island Rapid Transit Railroad and a stadium for the original New York Metropolitans were devised by Erastus Wiman. *From* An Illustrated Sketch Book of Staten Island, *1886.*

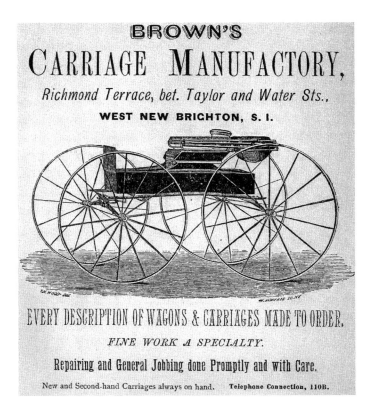

West New Brighton was better known for business activity than for crime. Brown's Carriage Manufactory and the Staten Island Printing and Dyeing Establishment were two successful concerns. *From* An Illustrated Sketch Book of Staten Island, *1886.*

in Clifton, presented New York governor David B. Hill with a petition of over one thousand signatures demanding that Barbour be liberated. Citing Barbour's act as being one of self-defense, both the reverend and Wiman requested that the sentence be commuted to the six months already served. They stressed that Barbour had never been involved in any unlawful conduct. It took Hill quite some time, but he finally transmitted a pardon on September 7, 1886. Barbour had lost almost eleven months of his life for defending himself against a bully and a maniac.

Top: Businessman Erastus Wiman made every effort to have his employee Ferrand Barbour released from jail for killing Edward Drurer. *From* Chances of Success, *1893.*

Right: Reverend Dr. John Eccleston of Saint John's Church gathered one thousand signatures on a petition calling for the release of Ferrand Barbour. *From* History of Richmond County, Staten Island, *1887.*

CHAPTER 6

DUELING: WITH KEEN-EDGED SPADES

Some called them communists; some called them religious fanatics. They denied both labels. Referring to their group as the Straight Edge Society, they were also known as "A School of Methods for the Application of the Teachings of Jesus to Business and Society."[40] Even though they lacked a catchy and uncomplicated alternate name, they did have simple beginnings. In 1899, four men down on their luck met while living at the Hotel Mills in Manhattan. They discussed varying principles and a way of life that intersected social justice and business that profited to provide for all. By 1901, their growing unit occupied the entire fourth floor of 640 Sixth Avenue in that borough, where they lived by the "Golden Rule." Since some of the original members were experienced printers, printing was their first enterprise. They took in job printing, published a newsletter called the *Straight Edge* and distributed a number of self-published booklets—none of which was copyrighted, since they wanted others to benefit from what they created for their own livelihood. The *Straight Edge* was available by subscription, with the price calculated to cover the cost of paper, ink, postage and thirty-five cents an hour for the mechanical and clerical labor necessary to produce the publication. "If the receipts exceed the cost of these items the surplus is divided amongst the subscribers. If they fall short the subscribers are apprised of the deficiency and those who wish to apply the Golden Rule do so."[41] Paid advertising space was not an option. Furthermore, the colony believed it was easier and less expensive to forgive debts rather than to keep books.

The Straight Edge Society's next attempt at commercial effort was baking. It was largely successful. By March 1901, two to three hundred loaves of wheat and corn bread were produced daily. While each man had a time card and hours were recorded, extra compensation in any form was not a reward for working harder or longer hours. Members were welcome to inform others if they were "not laboring for the best results." The advised individual was free to accept the advice or disregard it as he saw fit. If a rich man were to join the society, his money might not be put in the treasury but rather used for tools or equipment. Members lived only on what was earned by the membership. Their most important bylaws stated:

> *Thou shalt love thy neighbor like thyself.*
> *In honor preferring one another.*
> *Lay not up for yourself treasures upon earth.*
> *I am in the midst of you as he that serveth.*
> *Take heed that ye do not your righteousness before men to be seen of them.*[42]

The group was expanding. More than twenty-two acres of Rossville farmland on Staten Island was selected for the next Straight Edge altruistic endeavor. It was leased from James Winant on April 1, 1901, and was to be called "The Land of the Living."[43] There was no plan to move the entire Manhattan colony to Rossville. The group had no interest in being set apart from society and shunning civilization (per the *Sun*, which obviously had some ridiculous but not necessarily uncommon ideas about Staten Island's isolation); only sixteen men, women and children were to relocate to the Staten Island settlement. They were simply entering new areas of labor that were to include truck farming, small-scale iron working and manufacturing acetylene gas machines. On this acreage, they would also grow the needed fruits and vegetables for a restaurant at the Manhattan site. Already existing on this acreage were three barns, a greenhouse, a fruit orchard and a mansion.

The society's chief (although no one was so designated) or "go-to" man was Wilbur F. Copeland, who explained that it had twelve rooms on Sixth Avenue. One man made the beds, one man scrubbed the floors, one man dusted, one man washed the dishes and so on. At Rossville, Copeland hoped to establish a "school of cooperative industry" where a thorough training in mechanical and industrial arts would be received. The agricultural efforts would include dairy and poultry yards and a truck garden. An onsite power plant would fuel a foundry, machine shop, laundry, woodworking factory

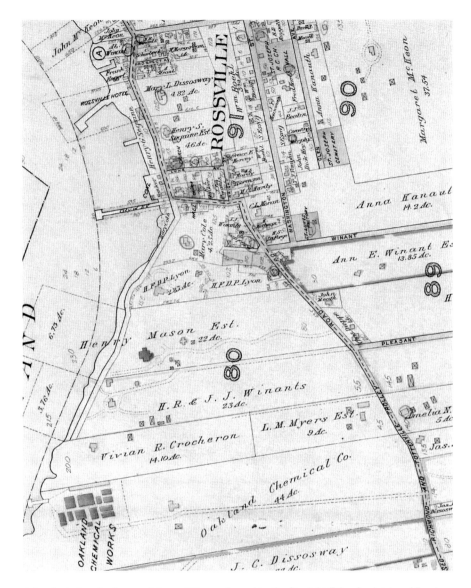

Atlas depicting the farms of James Winant (leased to the Straight Edge Society) and Louis Meyers. *From the* E. Robinson Atlas, Borough of Richmond, City of New York, *1907.*

and other industries. Living accommodations for fifty to one hundred people would be built, with more to follow. The Rossville farm was to be self-sustaining. According to Copeland, one of the principal endeavors of the Straight Edge Society was to provide work for the unemployed.

However, thus far they had "avoided publicity in order to be free from a host of possibly undesirable applicants."[44] Copeland also pointed out that the money possessed by such men as Andrew Carnegie or David Rockefeller really belonged "to the world at large." The society called for applying the laws of love to all human activity. All individuals of good character were invited to join the Straight Edge Society.

One journalist noted that these "ethereal folk" had "clean table linen but not always clean faces, and they remind one of Tennyson's 'mild-eyed, melancholy Lotos-Eaters' in a land where all things always seem the same… their law of cooperation frowns upon any rash soul who tries to escape the monotonous routine of simple, personal labor, and attempts to accomplish greater things by more radical means."[45]

In a newspaper interview, a member was asked what would become of the members when they were too old to work. He responded that this issue had not yet been encountered. The group would deal with such a situation when it arose. That was how the Straight Edge Society functioned. It dealt with problems as they came up and did not worry about possible future dilemmas.

By March 28, 1901, the society had grown to sixteen individuals, including several women. Newspaper coverage had brought additional members, and four applications were being processed. Copeland was of the belief that all were happy, hopeful and content.

The first of June saw twenty men, women and children living at the Sixth Avenue quarters. The restaurant, known as the Straight Edge Club-Room, was open for business. Printed atop the menu was the statement "Nothing That Ever Squealed," as all offerings were free of meat. Fried sweet potatoes, stewed corn, lettuce salad, bread and butter, apple pie, cheese, tea, coffee, cocoa and Postum cereal were available for the hungry. No charity was ever accepted, for the Straight Edgers did not believe in it. New plans called for a tailor shop, a boot and shoe shop and a hat factory in Manhattan. Sundays were spent at the Staten Island farm, with the hope that summer would allow all to take turns staying at Rossville.

The U.S. Department of Labor presented an August 1901 report by Reverend Dr. Alexander Kent on the Straight Edge. Describing the colony as living harmoniously, Reverend Kent wrote: "These people profess to believe it both possible and practical to apply in actual business and social affairs the principles enunciated in the Sermon of the Mount."[46] They were indeed living an uncomplicated life, as verified by an advertisement in the *Evening Telegram* of August 21, 1901. It read: "THIRTY old dollars to exchange for Laundry washer, Oakley preferred. STRAIGHT EDGE, Rossville, S.I."

All might have been going well at the Sixth Avenue location, but life at the Staten Island site was unraveling by the spring of 1902. Austin N. Donaldson had joined the Straight Edge Society the previous summer after resigning from his position as principal of a Highland, New York high school. Along with his wife and three children, Donaldson moved to the Staten Island outpost, where much of his farming activity focused on berry culture, including planting and raising raspberries and strawberries, for which the Rossville soil was well suited. Donaldson was also involved with "wetland mitigation" but in a very unharmonious way.

On the morning of Thursday, April 10, 1902, Austin Donaldson took a spade and clobbered neighbor Louis N. Meyers across the head. Meyers fell. He would soon be as dead as last year's leaf litter. Not only would Meyers die, but so, too, would the Golden Rule—for Austin Donaldson, anyway.

Life at the Rossville farm had become complex and was disintegrating, with some ruminating that both Donaldson and the farm were no longer a working component of the Straight Edge Society. Whatever schism took place during late 1901 resulted in the farm going under the supervision of Episcopalian minister Reverend Mr. Dalton of the Trinity Parish (who performed missionary work at Ellis Island on the side). Dalton joined the Straight Edge Society during the spring of 1901, and it was he who provided funding to lease the Rossville farm. Initially, there were twenty-two members at the site. Donaldson acceded to Dalton's request to manage the farm. The reverend dropped in now and again to check on farm business. He provided his own nightly accommodations by constructing his own onsite lodge.

Before his encounter with Donaldson's spade, Louis Meyers had resided at Rossville for the previous twenty years. He and his wife had eight children, the eldest twenty-three years old and the youngest five. Described as a "man of exemplary habits," he was a "total abstainer and never quarrelsome."[47] A swamp on Meyers's property seems to have been the root of all evil. It troubled Donaldson greatly that the wetland drained directly onto, and flooded, the land he so tenderly attended. Donaldson requested that Meyers remedy the continuous deluge onto his crops, and if he would not, Donaldson and his Straight Edge companions were only too happy to improve drainage conditions. Meyers's response is not known, but it obviously did not please Donaldson, who took it upon himself, according to the fine people of Rossville, to dig a series of ditches at the swamp, with the result that Meyers's own farm was inundated with swamp water. On April 10, Meyers, Donaldson and property owner James Winant met to discuss the situation. What transpired after the meeting was witnessed by Ralph Lake, a nineteen-year-old in Meyers's employ. Lake stated that he and Meyers went to the ditches dug by Donaldson, whereupon Meyers told Lake to fetch a spade so the two could fix Donaldson's offensive work. Meyers already had a shovel in hand. As Lake returned, he saw Donaldson, who had been working twenty-five feet from Meyers, run toward Meyers, who was bending over the ditch. When Donaldson reached Meyers, he took the spade in his hand and struck a blow to Meyers's head. Meyers collapsed, and Lake ran to get Mrs. Meyers. They returned to find Donaldson standing over the farmer's body. Mrs. Meyers asked Donaldson, "Who killed my husband?" Donaldson responded, "I did."[48] Donaldson might not have realized triumph at fixing floods, but he was quite a sensation at assaulting a man. He had successfully crushed the front of Meyers's skull. The farmer was removed to the S.R. Smith Infirmary at New Brighton, where he died two days later, never regaining consciousness.

Austin Donaldson was brought before Coroner Schaefer, who ordered him held without bail until an inquest was organized. Donaldson swore it was an accident but was advised that anything he said could be used against him. He quickly shut up. When told of the Staten Island event, Wilbur Copeland was quite surprised. As a side note, it seems that the Manhattan branch of the society was evaporating, too. By now, there were only four members, including Copeland and his wife. That was down from a high of sixty the previous summer.

Much excitement ensued at Donaldson's trial, especially on July 22, 1902. A close friend of Louis Meyers, Jacob Levy was raptly paying attention to the testimony of Ralph Lake while he described the hit taken by the well-liked farmer. Levy became agitated. His gasps for air resonated throughout the courtroom, and his head fell forward, as did he. Before court attendants reached him, he collapsed to the floor. A physician was summoned, and he declared the seventy-five-year-old dead from heart failure, brought on by excitement. The trial resumed thirty minutes later.

Surprise testimony came from Staten Island photographer Isaac Almsted, who had taken a series of images focusing on Meyers's farm. Almsted's photos were viewed by the participants, and the photographer was asked a number of questions about the proximity of the Meyers farm and the terrain of the Straight Edge, now referred to as the Golden Rule Farm.

Fifteen witnesses took the stand to vouch for Donaldson's good character. Many referred to him as a "serious, scholarly appearing man."[49] All were amazed when Donaldson swore under oath that Meyers struck him

Richmond County coroner George Schaefer (pictured above) ordered Austin Donaldson held in custody until the inquest of Louis Meyers's death was completed. *From* Prominent Men of Staten Island, *1893*.

first. Donaldson asserted that he was departing the scene before further escalation when he turned and saw Meyers and Lake filling the ditches he had previously dug to prevent the floods. As such, he returned to Meyers and was assaulted again. This caused Donaldson to "involuntarily" strike

BECOME AN ASSOCIATE

In the most interesting social experiment of modern times

The Straight Edge Industrial Settlement

No. ı Abingdon Square, New York City.

Advertisement for the Straight Edge Industrial Settlement, a later incarnation of the Straight Edge Society. *From the* Public, *no date.*

Logo of the Straight Edge Industrial Settlement. *From the* Public, *February 9, 1917.*

Meyers with his own spade. Donaldson called it "a reflex action of the nervous system."[50] He claimed he did not want to hit Meyers; he only wanted to knock the man's spade out of his hand. Reflex action or not (no doubt this was the first and last time this defense was used), Austin Donaldson was found guilty of manslaughter in the first degree by a jury of his peers. Judge Gaynor sentenced the lay minister to three years and six months in prison. Those who knew Donaldson insisted he did not kill Meyers. In fact, they noted, he was so gentle he would step to the side of a path rather than squish a worm underfoot. Said to be a man of culture and refinement, friends thought it important to note that Donaldson was descended from a long line of scholars, and his relations were above most. "His father was a graduate of Hamilton College and one of his brothers was a Presbyterian Minister," while another was Consul-General at Nicaragua.[51] None of this mattered. When the verdict was relayed to Mrs. Donaldson, she wept bitterly. Mrs. Meyers and her eight children were pleased. It seems that Donaldson expected a bad outcome from the trial, as he had a completed appeal application in his pocket. The appeal was quickly denied by Gaynor, who stated that Donaldson had a fair trial and was ably defended. Off to prison he went.

Back on the farm, Mrs. Donaldson and her three daughters dutifully tended the agricultural business, including raising popcorn, watermelon, sweet potatoes and other garden truck.

The year 1902 was not a pleasant one for property owner James Winant, nor was it a pleasant year for the woman he found floating in the Arthur Kill River off the shoreline of his Rossville farm. It was on July 25 that the awful discovery was made. Said to be young and handsome, there were no marks of violence on the body. About five feet tall, she had dark skin and hair and blue eyes and was about to become a mother. There was no identification found on her person.

By 1918, the Straight Edge Society was realizing financial difficulties. The following year, what was then known simply as the Straight Edge Baking Company was bankrupt. Wilbur Copeland died in Alpine, New Jersey, on July 31, 1943. The Golden Ruler was seventy-nine years old.

CHAPTER 7

DANCER WITH A WOODEN LEG (OR THE PRESENCE OF PREVALENT PREJUDICE IN THE ABSENCE OF POLITICAL CORRECTNESS)

Captain of Detectives Ernest L. Van Wagner had officers positioned all around Staten Island. They were watching every ferryboat landing—and there were several. There was not yet a bridge by which to exit or enter the island, but ferries did arrive and depart from Port Richmond, Old Place, Travis, Tottenville and St. George. To leave this island, you needed a boat or two very strong arms, which might not have been out of the question for the person Van Wagner sought. The captain had a particularly vicious double homicide to solve. The executioner needed to be apprehended—quickly.

It was early spring, just past daylight on April 6, 1923. On this pleasant, peaceful morning, milkman Walter Donovan was making daily deliveries to the thirsty people of Dongan Hills. Driving along a secluded stretch of Sea View Avenue, near a creek where bootleggers rendezvoused to commit lawless rumrunning activities, Donovan was shocked to see a discarded fur coat on the roadside. Jumping out of his Brighton Dairy Company delivery truck, he tugged on the fur. Much to his surprise, it moved and divulged a horribly mutilated woman coated in congealing blood. No sooner had this discovery been made then Donovan spotted another fur-clad woman ditched on the opposite side of the road! The terrified milkman sprinted to his truck and raced to the Stapleton police station.

Fashionably dressed in the styles of their day, these bobbed-haired women, both wearing silk clothing and fur coats, had been dead for only a short time. When police arrived, they were still warm to the touch. While these battered women were covered in blood, the ground surrounding them was not, leading police to theorize that they were murdered elsewhere and unceremoniously dumped in this isolated location. Not thirty feet from one of the bodies, a bloodied knife was located. Here was another interesting find: one of the women had an artificial leg! Police were very fortunate. A receipt for her wooden leg was found in the pocket of her fur coat. She was Irene Blandino of 77 Cole Street, Jersey City, New Jersey. The throats of both women had been slashed, as had their backs, between the shoulder blades. Their hands were covered with knife wounds, indicating they had attempted to grab the weapon from their attacker. One woman's wrists were lacerated. According to police, the struggle was so fierce that "their faces were distorted by fear and pain." Mrs. Blandino's jaw was actually "hacked away." The hair of both women "was a mass of tangled blood-clotted strands and rivulets of blood from their gaping wounds…traced ghastly patterns over their paled faces."[52] The medical examiner theorized that the two were murdered around 3:00 a.m. A resident who lived down the road corroborated that he heard an automobile around that time. Sea View Avenue led to a bungalow colony at Ocean Breeze. It was the perfect place for a fiendish murder or the deposit of two lifeless women, as it was a tiny cinder lane surrounded by marshes. There was little, if any, traffic.

Police investigators on both sides of the Kill Van Kull believed it was a Black Hand vendetta. The women had probably talked too much, and more than likely, the killings were related to the murder of Irene Blandino's husband (or one of her husbands), Frank Bongiovani. A hood, he had been executed in February 1921. The year before his death, Bongiovani was arrested in connection with the shooting of two men in Hudson County, New Jersey. Police stated that both Bongiovani and one of the bullet-riddled men were members of the mob and that the gunfire was the result of a feud between gangsters. After seven weeks, Bongiovani was released on bail. Thereafter, he met Irene, who was living with another man. She and Frank promptly married. But the man Irene was living with when she met Bongiovani would not have his honor besmirched by their marriage. He and a group of other villains set upon Bongiovani as he sat in a saloon. Stabbed numerous times, Bongiovani refused to disclose the name of the attacker to police. He simply stated, "I know what to do with him when I get out of here."[53] Irene also declined to tell police who initiated the assault. She knew that if she squealed, retaliation would arrive swiftly. Surprisingly, Bongiovani died from his wounds ten days later, and police never discovered the name of his slayer. Irene was little concerned with the murder. Six months later, she married James Blandino. Jersey City authorities were well aware of

Irene Blandino—her activities and the company she kept—as she was often observed with Black Hand members. James Blandino admitted that his wife was seldom home.

The other dead woman found at Dongan Hills was erroneously identified as Bessie McMahon, then Peggy McMahon and, later, Peggy Phillips. They were close. Her real name was Ethel Phillips. She was only eighteen years old. At the crime scene, the medical examiner stated that she was the most beautiful woman he ever saw (and that while she was coated in congealing blood).

James Blandino identified the body of his wife as it withered in the morgue. He informed the authorities that he had no knowledge whatsoever regarding the murders. When he spoke to police, he was accompanied by Rosario de Lorenzo, who both lived with the Blandinos and assisted James in the barbershop he owned. Both men had alibis for the time of the murder. Lest anyone think otherwise, these women were earmarked for murder. Neither was robbed of their jewelry, and Mrs. Blandino had fifty dollars on her person.

Detectives discovered that Irene Blandino was the daughter of a Utica, New York "fish monger" who had turned $1,380 over to her the previous year. It was money from the streetcar accident that took her leg at the age of eleven. It had been safeguarded until she reached the legal age of twenty-one. When word reached Utica that Irene was dead, information about her earlier life was revealed. Many were surprised to discover that her real name was Elvira Salerno Blandino and that she had been married three times. Her first husband was Benedeto Delicato, whom she had married at the age of fifteen. It was later claimed that the couple never legally divorced. Elvira left Utica, and her given first name, two years before the murder when she was nineteen. Her family complained that she was heard from infrequently. While in Utica, Irene was arrested twice: once in 1918 for shoplifting and once in 1920 for adultery, a charge for which she was exonerated. According to her father, Pasquale Salerno, James Blandino was very jealous where his wife was concerned. Salerno claimed that his daughter was "a very pretty girl with light hair, brown eyes" and "even teeth."[54] Her brother stated she was the prettiest girl in Utica. According to Pasquale, Elvira and James had separated for a while but had recently patched up their differences. As he sobbed bitterly, the dead girl's father lamented that she had promised to come home for Easter (April 1) but had not and that if she had, perhaps her end would not have been so tragic. Brother Joseph blamed James Blandino and his involvement with the Black Hand.

As a child, Elvira Salerno wanted only to have fun. She was "curious about life" and had "a gay always laughing nature."[55] Even after the streetcar accident, she remained upbeat. Her sense of amusement continued into adulthood, as she was often seen at dance halls; even with the loss of her leg, she managed to dance in a cabaret professionally. She loved parties, too, and would attend dances and other celebrations without her husband, which was, of course, scandalous at the time. Of her nightly activities, James Blandino commented that they were "gay and fevered."[56]

Police did know that Irene and Ethel had spent time in the company of twenty-one-year-old Alfred Montitaro as taxicab driver Joseph Portizo took the three for a ride Wednesday, April 4. On that evening, they visited Jersey City, Hoboken and Bayonne. One stop on this outing had the trio searching at a restaurant for a man named Eddie, but Eddie was not to be found that night. Portizo dropped the women off at the Blandino barbershop in Jersey City around 2:00 a.m. In addition to the barbershop, James Blandino was part owner of a Jersey City saloon. Around 8:00 p.m. the next night, Thursday, April 5, James was called from the barbershop to the saloon by his partner. When Blandino departed the barbershop, Irene and Ethel were in the rear of the building. De Lorenzo reported that after he closed the barbershop, the two women left with him. De Lorenzo had last seen them on a street corner as he headed to a nearby club. After closing the saloon, James Blandino arrived home around 2:00 a.m. Neither of the two women was in residence.

On April 7, 1923, James Blandino and Rosario de Lorenzo were arraigned in Stapleton Court by Magistrate William Fetherstone on manslaughter charges in the deaths of Irene Blandino and Ethel Phillips. After removal to the West Brighton Station, the two barbers were interrogated for several hours by detectives from the "Italian squad" (political correctness would take decades to arrive).[57] Meanwhile, every bungalow dweller from Midland Beach to New Dorp Beach was questioned about the double homicide. According to police, "every spaghetti palace, of which there are several down farther on Southfield Boulevard, speak-easy and delicatessen" was entered.[58] Owners and customers were interviewed for clues as to how and why these women were dumped dead on Sea View Avenue. No one knew, saw or heard a thing. When closely examined, the murder weapon was said to be a five-inch skinner's knife. Still intact even though it was involved in a ferocious mêlée, the blood-covered blade still held a price tag, indicating it was a new purchase. Cost: thirty-five cents.

Police subsequently picked up Alfred Montitaro, the Jersey City longshoreman who drove around with the women the night before their disappearance. He stated that Irene and Ethel were not too "particular as to how they became acquainted with men." As a matter of fact, "he picked them up," and they walked along the street until the cabbie gave them a lift.[59] Another clue came in from Elias Ginsburg, who saw two women and three men on a Staten Island ferry on Thursday, April 5. The women fit the descriptions of Irene and Ethel. All appeared to have been drinking. Staten Island cab driver William Stiering said he drove three "swarthy men" and two women from the St. George Ferry Terminal to Liberty Avenue and Southfield Avenue in Dongan Hills "shortly after 12 o'clock Friday morning." He viewed the bodies of Irene and Ethel at the morgue and "partly" identified them as his passengers.[60] Police narrowed their search to men bearing scratched faces, as human flesh was found under the fingernails of the deceased. Cars with possible bloodstains were also sought.

Jersey City authorities believed that Irene and Ethel had information or were involved in bootlegging, which, according to Police Chief Battersby, was "composed principally of Italians who operated between the island and points in New Jersey."[61] The chief did not associate the murder with any love interests or jealousy. Regarding Ethel Phillips, also referred to as Peggy on occasion, police ascertained that she was a Bayonne, New Jersey resident who had recently been released from the House of the Good Shepherd of Hudson County, where she had been "committed" by her parents for running away from home. In addition, Bayonne chief of police Patrick O'Neill discovered that Irene and Ethel were involved in a "heated argument" with two (again) Italian men in an automobile on Hudson Avenue in Bayonne on Thursday, April 5. They further uncovered the fact that the "Eddie" Ethel sought in the restaurant was actually a "Joe."[62] As such, law enforcement began hunting for the two men and for the elusive Joe. Police now held the opinion that these three men killed the women, although it was probably not their intention to kill Ethel. Her execution occurred so she could not bear witness against the executioner. Another sensational theory that attracted widespread attention suggested that "the women were murdered as the climax of a wild orgy staged in one of the cottages" at a Staten Island beach.[63]

Meanwhile, back on Staten Island, the district attorney of Richmond County was actively seeking Irene Blandino's first husband, Benedeto Delicato, while James Blandino, Irene's third husband was still held in the Staten Island jail. Authorities were convinced James knew more about Irene's murder than he was willing to acknowledge. They believed he was afraid. If he revealed the truth, he would become the victim of a contract killing as well.

All were perplexed when an attempted break-in occurred at the morgue where Irene and Ethel were being held. According to night watchman Frank Ford, on April 8, two dark, well-dressed men drove up in a touring car and attempted to access the building through a window. When Ford went to the door, the men endeavored to push past him. He succeeded in striking one across the head with his nightstick. They turned and fled by automobile.

More oddities about this already unusual case were revealed when detectives discovered that Irene Blandino was friends with Charles Ponzi, "the notorious 'frenzied financer,'" also known as the "Bushel Basket Millionaire." While living in Boston and working as a cabaret dancer (despite her artificial leg), Irene met and became fast friends with Ponzi. Whether Irene was involved in Ponzi schemes was never made clear, but she was so well known on the Boston dance circuit she was dubbed the "Italian Florrie."[64]

The dancing Mrs. Blandino also befriended a man named Di Pasquali, who police later announced was with the two women the day they died. Detectives received a tip that the "roughly dressed young Italian" Di Pasquali had accompanied the women to the Mechanics and Manufacturers Bank in Union Hill, New Jersey, where Irene withdrew $100 from an account in the name of Irene Bova.[65]

On April 10, 1923, Rosario de Lorenzo was finally discharged from jail. Police acknowledged he knew nothing about the murders. The following day, Ethel Phillips's remains were released from the morgue and interred at Lake Cemetery in Graniteville, while Irene Blandino's body languished without any attempts to claim her. The morgue keeper finally announced that if her body were not removed soon, it would be given a lonely burial at the Farm Colony Potter's Field, as was the policy for remains left more than a week. The recently released James Blandino finally requested Irene's body, and a simple, inexpensive interment was to take place on April 14 at Ocean View Cemetery in Oakwood.

The authorities soon announced that Irene Blandino's first husband, Benedeto Delicato, was finally located. Found in Cortland, New York, police interviewed him there on April 16. Claiming that Irene left him, Delicato stated he had not seen her since the day of her departure.

Almost three weeks after Irene Blandino was buried in an austere Oakwood grave, James Blandino was arrested again. This time, Jersey City detectives charged him with perjury. It seems he visited two banks that held Irene's streetcar accident award. As he attempted to withdraw her money, Blandino claimed to be Irene's only living relative and next of kin. The Salernos of Utica balked at this effort and stated that the two were not even legally married. Next up was first husband, Benedeto Delicato, who had since remarried without a divorce from Irene. He descended upon the court as a claimant for the two New Jersey bank accounts held in Irene's name. As *Staten Island Advance* columnist Jack Reycraft later wrote, there were two claims by "two loving husbands" for the cash "but the barest, coldest funeral possible for the girl who left it!"—the woman who barely missed burial in a potter's field!

Walking alone along a lonely stretch of Vista Avenue in Dongan Hills on December 4, 1923, Ralph Fernatti was on his way to grammar school when he discovered a murdered man who had been stabbed in the right side of the neck. The killer(s) had severed his jugular vein, broken several ribs, pierced his liver and given the deceased a vicious beating. A signet ring with the initials "P.C." and a diamond ring adorned his fingers. Short with a dark complexion, it was certainly not surprising when police claimed that he was "probably an Italian."[66] He was well trimmed with apparel that included a pinstriped black suit, patent leather shoes and silk socks—even his underwear was new and stylish. The body was discovered not two miles from where murdered bootlegger Frederick Eckert had been found with a six bullets in his brain on August 21, 1920, and not one mile from where the unfortunate Irene Blandino and Ethel Phillips were unceremoniously dumped the previous spring. Police thought this mystery man's murder was the result of a bootlegging battle. Bootlegging or not, this was evolving into a very trendy location for disposing the illegally dead.

CHAPTER 8

A RUM RAID GONE AWRY

As the steam lighter pulled up to the New Brighton dock of the Tanner-Gross Milling Company, four men readied themselves to jump ashore. It was March 2, 1922. The crooks were hoping for a profitable evening. The plan was to steal $35,000 worth of stored legal government-bonded liquor. It was the era of Prohibition—liquor, government approved or not, was difficult to come by.

As they rapped on the warehouse entrance, one of the thugs held a blackjack. When night watchman Michael Connor opened the door, he was clubbed into insensibility. After lingering for seven arduous days, Connor succumbed to the splintering of his skull on March 9, 1922. Michael Connor was slain for attempting to protect thirty barrels of whiskey.

The bonded booze was stored in a warehouse at the bottom of Jersey Street on Richmond Terrace. Tanner-Gross actually rented the site to the C.O. Rudolph Warehouse Company, which was legally responsible for safeguarding the liquor. Nine men were arrested in connection with the theft and murder. The scoundrels were said to be members of a New York City bootleg ring that regularly dealt in illicit swindles—some netting millions of dollars. Frank Bickford, Eugene Merrell, Frank Storey, John Green and Rensselaer Carney were charged with conspiracy. Raymond Collins, James Pymm, Frank Brown and Joseph Gonigle were charged with conspiracy and murder. It was Merrell who captained the boat along the Kill Van Kull and then removed the criminals after their felonious activities.

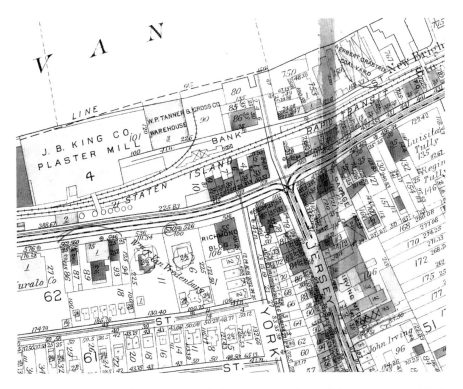

Location of the Tanner-Gross warehouse in New Brighton, where Michael Connor was killed. *From the* G.W. Bromley Atlas of the City of New York, Borough of Richmond, *1917.*

Gonigle, Merrell and Brown were Staten Island residents; the others lived in Brooklyn and only descended upon Staten Island for robbery and murder. Bickford wasted no time in announcing that he was related to Brooklyn borough president Edward J. Reigelmann, who at first denied any familial connection. The politician finally admitted, or was informed, that Bickford was married to a sister of his sister-in-law. (Not exactly kissing cousins, but it was important to Bickford for obvious reasons.)

Richmond County district attorney Joseph Maloy claimed that this was just the beginning of exposing the most significant whiskey ring in New York City. Chief of Detectives Van Wagner of Staten Island reported that one of the hoodlums was "ready to sign a confession naming financial backers of the alleged bootleg band" and that disclosure would "create a city-wide sensation."[67] After the criminal raid and murder, the prized legitimate liquor was moved to an unknown storage location.

Raymond Collins was the first thug brought to trial for slaughtering the night watchman. Each of the defendants requested a separate trial, which did not please the public since it would cost the borough $150,000. Former Richmond County district attorney Frank Innes defended Collins, while Judge J. Harry Tiernan presided over the court proceedings. The trial opened on April 17, 1922, with District Attorney Maloy dramatically declaring that he was in possession of facts that would "go a long way in exposing the most vicious band of bootleggers in Greater New York who would not stop at murder to accomplish their purpose."[68] Maloy further proclaimed that "they hold human life so cheaply they believed they could go on forever defying law and order in their desire to obtain whiskey."[69] Judge Tierney planned evening sessions during the Collins trial. Since the jurors would be "locked up" at night, he ordered that they be taken on hour-long automobile drives during their dinner break. Motoring excursions would move through the island "so they could get the air" to "fit them for a long night's session."[70] Rensselaer Carney (certainly a mobster with a memorable name) took the stand as a witness for the state against his former partners in crime. Carney was the gangster who, prior to the night of the robbery, discovered that a night watchman was stationed on the premises. He claimed that when he discovered this fact, he quit the operation, making one wonder why he was with the raiding partying the night of the Staten Island invasion.

On April 21, 1922, Raymond Collins was convicted of killing the unsuspecting Michael Connor. Defying his lawyer's advice, Collins took the stand in his own defense. While under cross-examination, he was forced to admit that yes, he was an ex-convict and that yes, he was currently out of prison on a suspended conviction for passing a worthless check in the amount of $11,000. Oh, and not only was it a bad check, but it was also a bounced payment for a bootlegging transaction! Collins was a fascinating criminal and informed his captive courthouse audience that he was once a steward at the St. Regis Hotel and that he sang and illustrated songs in movie theaters. Quite a colorful life, but there was more: he was also a graduate of Dartmouth University. None of this trivia mattered, as the case fell apart for Collins when he admitted that he was the individual knocking on the warehouse door when Michael Connor answered. It was an efficient jury, countering with a conviction of first-degree murder for college grad Raymond Collins in just one hour and fifteen minutes. Collins was sentenced to death by electrocution at Sing Sing. In response, he declared his innocence and then pleaded that Gonigle, Brown and Pymm be given clemency. When asked why he did not plead guilty to murder in the second degree like co-defendant Frank Brown,

Raymond Collins was remanded to Sing Sing Prison to await electrocution for the murder of Michael Connor. *Library of Congress.*

Collins responded that he was not guilty of murder in any degree. Brown was sentenced to twenty years to life at Sing Sing Prison for his participation. Collins was confident he would win an appeal.

Joseph Gonigle was offered twenty years to life if he would plead guilty to murder in the second degree, but he swore innocence and opted for a trial—this after a long consultation with his mother. District Attorney Maloy refused to give the deal to James Pymm. Claiming that Pymm knew the identity of three other individuals involved, who were still on the loose, Maloy informed Pymm he would get the offer when he provided their names and hiding places. Pymm refused, insisting that he would be dead as a doormat if he revealed their identities and location. Maloy responded that it was Pymm who actually hired the man who killed Connors—thus, Maloy believed Collins was innocent! James Pymm was clearly troubled. With tears in his eyes, he jumped to his feet and shouted, "For God's sake, let me tell what I know. I don't want to die in the electric chair!"[71] After Pymm's counsel consulted with the district attorney, and with Maloy satisfied he would get the fugitives' names, he gave Pymm the chance to plead guilty to murder in the second degree. Rumors had circulated that Pymm would break down and divulge the information, hence the court was overflowing with more than five hundred in attendance when these spectacular events occurred. Extra security in the form of forty deputy sheriffs and six court officers were brought in to scrutinize the crowd. A dusting of detectives was dispersed throughout the courtroom as well. It was feared that an attempt would be made on Pymm's person. Tiernan called for Pymm and Gonigle's conveyance to Sing Sing at once. It was time for these two to begin serving their sentences. Deemed the "most dramatic scene ever witnessed in a Staten Island court room" by one Manhattan newspaper, the surprising revelations continued.[72] The next startling announcement revealed that St. Peter's Roman Catholic Church altar and choirboy Joseph Gonigle was to be murdered the night of the robbery! Given $15,000 to set up the theft at the warehouse, once the plan was successfully completed, the gunmen were going to shoot and kill the nineteen-year-old and keep the $15,000 themselves. Killing Gonigle would further ensure that his mouth would be sealed—forever. Fortunately, this portion of the evening's itinerary was not executed.

Said to be the "most learned inmate of the Sing Sing death house," Raymond Collins had "added luster to his name" when he won the condemned men's checkers championship in November 1922.[73] Housed in a circle of cells, the inmates were not allowed visual contact with one another. They did manage to play checkers with numbered board squares. All inmates were silent except the two contenders, who called their moves aloud. Referred to "as the least coveted title" in the world, no one thought for even one second that death house checkers would gain in popularity.[74]

Sing Sing checkers champion Collins received even better news the following month, when the Court of Appeals overturned his conviction and granted him a new trial in the murder of Michael Connors. Upon arrival at the Richmond County Courthouse in St. George, the first person to greet him was his wife. The trial was granted on the grounds that Judge Tierney erred when charging the jury. On June 14, 1923 Raymond C. Collins was acquitted of murdering Michael Connor. When the jury's verdict was read, Collins supposedly grabbed District Attorney Joseph Maloy's hand and exclaimed, "Twelve honest men have declared that I did not murder the watchman."[75] Maloy was not done with Collins, though. He had Collins remanded to jail for ten days while he went before a grand jury for an indictment against Collins on a charge of conspiring to steal liquor. Meanwhile, the killer who took Michael Connor's life that hapless night has never been adequately identified.

CHAPTER 9

PLACED IN JEOPARDY—NIGHTLY

Friday, October 22, 1920—two young boys and a dog were ambling along upper Oakland Avenue near Forest Avenue in West New Brighton when they were shocked to discover the body of an unresponsive woman on an undeveloped tract of property. A two-foot-long hempen cord was proficiently wound around her throat. When police arrived, they surmised that the strangled woman was killed elsewhere since there was no evidence of a struggle where the body was dumped. "The high brush wasn't trampled" until later, when "crowds of curious arrived at the scene."[76] Authorities believed that after her untimely death, the woman was dragged over a rough wagon road, as she bore briar scratches and deep cuts across her hips. Law enforcement was working nonstop to identify the corpse when a man walked into the Stapleton morgue where the body was laid out for autopsy. He took one look at her and firmly stated that it was his wife, twenty-four-year-old Jennie Kussell. Speaking in broken English, Michael Kastanty, or Kussell (the English translation for Kastanty), had last seen his wife on Saturday, October 16, 1920. He lamented that she often disappeared, sometimes for days at a time. Her activities, police believed, "placed her in jeopardy…nightly."[77] The young woman with the blonde bob haircut was associated with men who carelessly displayed considerable amounts of money and who "were given to midnight riding in automobiles."[78] On most nights, she left the couple's 439 York Avenue home in Jersey City around 9:00 p.m. She claimed that she worked as a "scrub woman" in the Pulitzer Building on Park Row in Manhattan from midnight to 4:00 a.m., but police learned she had previously quit that cleaning job. Mrs. Kussell had, in fact, "turned to other pursuits" and "knew many men."[79] Mr. Kussell stated that, try as he might, she refused to stay home with him and their two children: Jennie, age six, and Fannie, age four. The youngsters were often cared for by neighbors, and they were actually playing in the street when one of the older neighborhood kids informed little Jennie that her mother had been found dead with a rope around her neck in a Staten Island lot.

When Michael last saw Jennie, she informed him that she was leaving to respond to a newspaper ad for a job. He knew she was lying. Kussell was well aware that she associated with unsavory characters from the Greenville section of Jersey City. On Sunday, October 19, he went to the police precinct to discuss her absence, but officers refused to respond when they heard that she frequently took off of her own free will. When Jersey City neighbors informed him that a dead woman bearing a resemblance to his wife was found on Staten Island, Michael headed to the Stapleton morgue for his own investigation.

In examining crime records, Jersey City police uncovered the fact that Mrs. Kussell had made a complaint against forty-eight-year-old Max Phillips of Varick Street, Jersey City, on September 28. Phillips had insulted her at 5:00 a.m. that morning. Later that day, it was reported that Phillips was viciously assaulted and beaten by three men. Further investigation revealed that Phillips had a serious fascination with Jennie Kussell. Oftentimes, he requested that they run away together.

When Mrs. Kussell was found dead, a wedding ring, a diamond ring, two plain gold rings and a platinum brooch holding seventeen pearls were missing from the body, leading police to initially believe she was the victim of a robbery that led to murder. But on March 16, 1921, a hood named James Gargone stated under oath that Mrs. Kussell lived in the home of condemned murderer Frank McNally and his wife on Staten Island and that her death was connected with the shooting of bootlegger Frederick Eckert, who had been found dead at Arrochar on August 21, 1920. These allegations were never proven, and more importantly, her murderer was never apprehended. One local columnist wrote in 1951: "The slaying of the pretty young cleaning woman who deserted her mop and pail for adventures that proved fatal may never be avenged."[80] It appears that this insight remains true to this day.

CHAPTER 10

A FORMER CABARET BEAUTY AND HER DASHING YOUNG SERGEANT

The butt end of a .45-caliber Smith and Wesson "regulation army pistol" provided the black eye and breast bruises on Elsie Smith. It had also provided the bullet that was shot into her brain. It was the identity of the individual who inflicted the bullet and the bruises that provided the mystery.

Elsie Smith was found dead on her bed by three men attached to the First Tank Corps at Miller Field, a small military base at New Dorp Beach, on January 3, 1932. They were dispatched when neighbor Agnes Ryan reported that Mrs. Smith had not been seen since January 1, when she, Elsie and Elsie's husband, Sergeant Albert L. Smith, had played a few rounds of cards on New Year's Eve. Mrs. Ryan left the couple around 1:00 a.m., and both were in fine spirits. When Inspector Ernest Van Wagner, a very busy man, arrived on the scene, he found that a fierce struggle had taken place in the barracks apartment. Chairs and a table were broken. Someone had even made an unsuccessful attempt at hiding one very important clue. The bedroom floor had been hastily mopped to remove an unknown substance(s).

Sergeant Albert Smith was actually stationed at Camp Dix in Wrightstown, New Jersey, where he was attached to the ordnance department. In charge of all rifles and pistols at the camp, Smith was on a four-day leave when his wife was found battered and lifeless on Staten Island.

Agnes Ryan reported hearing gunfire around 5:00 a.m. on New Year's Day but thought that perhaps it was simply a falling can of ashes. But the tenant above Ryan, Sergeant Richard LaFord, also reported hearing what he believed was a gunshot. The apartment above the Smiths was unoccupied.

A military base murder can be handled by army officials, but Miller Field commander Colonel W.G. McKee turned the case over to local civilian authorities, who immediately called for a widespread manhunt to find Sergeant Smith. An inspection of the apartment revealed that Smith's civilian clothes were missing but that his uniform was neatly hung in the couple's closet. Authorities dragged the ocean off Miller Field with the hope that the murder weapon would be recovered. Maybe the sergeant's body would be recovered, too? Several soldiers reported seeing Smith at the shoreline on the morning of January 2.

Originally from Tomlov, Russia, Elsie Smith had been married before. In 1914, she married Ivan Holesov in Siberia. Conflicting reports on how Elsie and Albert met circulated, but it seems they married while Smith was on duty with the Fifteenth Army Infantry in Tientsin, China, in 1925. He was described as tall, dark and handsome. A very pleasant man, he was said to have "an affectionate and worthy character." Albert L. Smith had joined the U.S. Army around 1924. Since that time, he had a developed a sterling service record. Known as a homebody, he had accumulated a considerable savings with both a Staten Island bank and the army paymaster.

Since none existed on Staten Island, Mrs. Smith attended the Russian Orthodox church in Ozone Park, New York. One of the congregation elders, M.C. Krietsky, was called to give testimony before a grand jury concerning Mrs. Smith's death. At this time, Krietsky stated that Mrs. Smith had come to him for counseling. She wanted to discuss with her husband facts about her earlier life that she had not previously disclosed to him. Krietsky told her to leave well enough alone and not inform him of past occurrences or activities. Elsie seems to have disregarded his advice and told her husband that she had been married to Holesov in Russia. In addition, she informed Albert that she had been a cabaret dancer in Russian clubs. It was quickly assumed that this information so enraged Smith that he beat Elsie without mercy and then shot and killed her. Others considered that Smith might have angered someone while on duty in the Far East, and perhaps that person or persons had come to the United States and killed his wife—and perhaps this mystery assailant had done away with Smith as well? Still another theory was heralded by Elsie's close friend Elizabeth Boenin, who stated that Albert Smith was livid with his wife for refusing to withdraw the money to buy his military discharge.

Police received a surprising report from a potential witness who saw Albert Smith leaving town on the evening of January 3. This person concluded that Smith was heading to a former residence in Benicia, California. In addition to being wanted for questioning related to his wife's murder, by January 7,

Smith was considered AWOL (absent without leave) from the army. Uncle Sam was now involved in the hunt. It was soon proven that Smith was not in California, as on March 6, the sergeant was apprehended on Staten Island. He certainly had not traveled far. None of the reasons proposed for Elsie's horrific death were correct, either. Smith admitted killing his wife but said it was to prevent her from living at Camp Dix. According to Smith, it was "a terrible place" and unfit for a woman. Ironically, the army had no plans to send Mrs. Smith to Camp Dix. Furthermore, Albert Smith's plans included killing himself on New Year's Day. A few days before commencement of his four-day leave, Smith was put in charge of the ordnance department, where he found the accounts muddled. He became so upset by the discrepancies that he opted for suicide; however, he admitted that he did not have the nerve to carry out his plan after killing his wife. It was also discovered that after the murder, Smith took his night's sleep next to her dead body.

During his time on the lam, Smith stayed at a lower East Side Manhattan mission under the name Martin Jacques. When he was arrested at Eighth Street and New Dorp Lane in New Dorp, he claimed to be heading to the police precinct to surrender. Because the murder had occurred on an army reservation, Smith faced a hanging if found guilty. Smith was held at the Richmond County Jail, where the physicians examining him came to a not-so-startling conclusion: he had a "mental disturbance." Even so, he was charged with murder in the first degree. The charge of army desertion, punishable by a court-martial, was put on hold for the time being.

Before the murder trial, Smith had what was then referred to as "a lunacy trial," in which psychiatrists for both the defense and the prosecution agreed. Albert Smith was insane. This was not the end of the matter, though, as a twelve-member jury still had to decide whether Smith was mentally balanced. In the courtroom, Smith was described as being continuously distracted. When asked to take the stand, he refused. It took a considerable amount of coaxing by both court and counsel for him to relent and go before the court. When questioned, he would silently move his lips. Five or more minutes later, he would speak his answers out loud. It came out that Smith's real last name was Zorhyde. He had changed it after bullies called him "sore hide." Smith had also been teased about his big feet since infancy, and his psychiatrist, Dr. Frank G. Young, stated that this was "the foundation upon which rests a present mental unbalance."[81]

The jury ruled that Albert L. Smith was insane and that he should be committed to an institution. Judge Moskowitz, who presided over the case, "declared the verdict the only one possible."[82]

Elsie Smith was waked at W.C. McCallum's in Great Kills and buried at Cypress Hills National Cemetery in Brooklyn. In later years, it was written that both the sergeant and Mrs. Smith were murdered by the same person. This reportedly occurred because neighbor Ryan claimed to have heard someone tinkering with the Smiths' furnace around daybreak, the same time Elsie was murdered. It was also announced that the burnable parts of Sergeant Smith's body were consumed in the furnace, while the murderer buried the skull and bones at some isolated south shore location. This is ridiculous for a number of reasons, the most obvious of which was the fact that Albert Smith was not dead. Also, if Mrs. Ryan was alert enough to hear the tinkering, she no doubt would have smelled burning flesh, as would the other tenants in the building. Aside from Mrs. Smith's brutal death, one important question does linger: why would someone like Sergeant Albert Smith be put in charge of an ordnance department?

CHAPTER 11

UNANSWERED FOR
EIGHTY-THREE YEARS

Nothing ever happened in Tottenville—or so people thought. Yes, there were occasional floods and Indian arrowheads found, but a murder? A sudden, and severe, reversal in thought occurred when Patrick Moore, on a day's outing from Brooklyn, took notice of a foot protruding through the brush as he passed through a thicket between Aspinwall Street and Finlay Avenue on June 7, 1931. Police were quickly notified. Upon their arrival, they realized the woman had been murdered and that she had been dead for several weeks. Assistant medical examiner Mandell Jacobi was also on the job, and he announced that the cause of death would be unknown until an autopsy was completed. Inspector Ernest Van Wagner believed the victim had been strangled. (Decades later, it was erroneously stated that the medical examiner was being cagey and actually did know what had killed the woman. This report further stated that her throat had been cut so deeply that the "head was almost severed from her body."[83] This was untrue.)

In addition to the thick brush, a blue *crêpe de chine* dress covered her body. This led police to believe she was Lillian Prehn, who had gone missing on March 29. Miss Prehn never returned to her 87 State Street home in West New Brighton after leaving her nursing job at 6:00 p.m. that day. According to one newspaper, she was "a friend of men" stationed at the U.S. Coast Guard base on the east shore of Staten Island. (Why is it that murdered men are never the "friends of women"?) Police questioned a number of individuals stationed at the base.

All were surprised when Lillian Prehn was found murdered in Tottenville, a quiet community better known for the historic Billopp House (pictured above). *From* History of Richmond County, after 1850.

Sadly, it was Lillian's distraught mother who made the initial identification when police arrived at her home with a strip of her missing daughter's dress. The grief-stricken mother also informed authorities that Lillian had a new dental bridge in her upper jaw. This fact verified that Lillian was the deceased. Robbery was not a motive, as the young woman wore two handsome rings, one of which appeared to have diamonds. Van Wagner theorized that she was murdered elsewhere and discarded at Tottenville or that she had been lured to the remote area and slain on site. He speculated that the dead woman's body could have been driven to the remote location via Hylan Boulevard, or it arrived by boat at the Aspinwall Street shoreline. Either scenario would have lent the killer a remote location at which to dispose of the remains. Richmond County district attorney Albert C. Fach immediately interviewed four U.S. Coast Guardsmen stationed on Staten Island. Two seamen were even recalled from sixty miles at sea. Alvin Smith refused to answer many of the questions presented. He was to be interrogated a second time. Three guardsmen—Douglas Walsh, George Talbot and Arthur Millard—were cleared of any involvement. While suspicion was placed on Smith, police noted he had gone to sea two days before Lillian's disappearance and had not returned until April 10. One of the sailors was a former sweetheart, but he had quarreled with Lillian's mother during the courtship and was thus forbidden to see Lillian again. Questioned by police, he claimed to have not seen Lillian since the fight and further stated that he had been transferred to a base down south. When he returned, he did attempt to contact Lillian. It was then that he discovered she was missing.

Lillian's family believed that the killer was someone their daughter knew. The police investigation was at a standstill. Their hopes were raised when they discovered that Lillian kept a diary. Perhaps it would provide clues to the killer's identity. However, the diary was nowhere to be found, nor was Lillian's handbag. No one could explain this heinous crime. That same year, detectives acknowledged that the murder of Lillian Prehn would never be unraveled. As of 2014, they are still correct.

CHAPTER 12

A CASE OF MURDER—A MOST BRUTAL ONE

This truly was a horror. The woman was splayed across the hotel room floor, her earrings ripped from her lobes and rings torn from her fingers. Beaten into submission, death had come from a sixteen-inch lead pipe. The victim had been frightfully battered. Her neck was shattered. With arms extended, as if warding off a blow, she was surrounded by blood, which saturated the carpet. Another pool of blood was found on the opposite side of the room. On a table in the center of the room stood an empty champagne bottle with two wine glasses. But it was hardly an evening of romance—or perhaps it was.

Despite all of the brutality committed, no one heard a sound—not the residents above her room nor those adjacent. The atrocity was not realized until the chambermaid arrived to perform her morning duties around 9:30 a.m. This unsuspecting housekeeper had no idea that entering Room 84 of the Grand Hotel that morning was going to change her life.

The dead woman had checked into the hotel, located on Broadway and Thirty-First Street in Manhattan, alone on August 15, 1898. She had dinner alone and then departed the hotel alone. But when she returned, around 5:00 or 6:00 p.m., she was accompanied by an unidentified male. Shortly thereafter, champagne was called for. Around 7:00 p.m., they left the hotel together. Observed upon their midnight return, the mystery man was glimpsed making a hasty exit from the hotel around 2:00 a.m.

The unfortunate woman registered as "E. Maxwell and wife, Brooklyn." "She was noticeably handsome, a pronounced blonde…tastefully dressed—wearing a light waist, a linen skirt, a green silk petticoat, and a straw hat trimmed with bright flowers. The clerk noticed that she wore large diamond earrings and a diamond ruby ring."[84] The man, who was now nowhere to be found, was described as dapperly dressed in a blue suit and straw hat. About thirty-five years old, he had a dark moustache.

When the maid, Mary Higgins, entered the room, the murder weapon was found alongside the victim's body. Who was this woman? A card in the pocket of her clothing revealed that she was actually Emeline Reynolds, twenty years old. Some people called her "Dolly." When told that her daughter was murdered, Cristina Reynolds became hysterical and shouted, "Oh, they have murdered my child for her money."[85]

Coroner Bausch determined that Emeline's death had occurred around 1:00 a.m. "Two lacerated scalp wounds, each about two inches in length, were found on the left side of the head, one just back of the apex of the skull and the other two inches further back. The weapon had not broken the skull. Death resulted from a fracture of one of the cervical vertebrae."[86] Investigators believed the victim received the first strike while reclining on a sofa. Staggering across the room, she collapsed to the floor and died. Tucked into her corset, police found a check for $13,000 drawn from the Garfield National Bank. It was endorsed by S.J. Kennedy. The card bearing her name also held an address and revealed the fact that she had taken lessons at the American Academy of Dramatic Art. Emeline Reynolds also sold books. Her move to Manhattan was noted by her former nosy Mount Vernon, New York neighbors, who "in the secrecy of their homes nodded to each other significantly and commented on the magnificence of Emeline Reynolds gowns. The neighbors had made up their minds before they saw her pony and cart, her bicycle and the carriage in which she frequently drove to her father's house that Emeline had changed."[87]

The previous weekend, Emeline had told her mother that she was going to withdraw money from the Mount Vernon Bank and then go to a dentist that Monday. Who this dentist was, Mrs. Reynolds had no idea. While the mother was talking to reporters about the murder, a telegram for Emeline arrived. It read: "Will call to-night. Have been very busy."[88] It was signed "M.B.M." Mrs. Reynolds did not know who sent the missive or what it meant.

Emeline was last seen by her maid on August 15 as she departed her 370 West Fifty-eighth Street apartment after 3:00 p.m. The maid, Margaret Adams, told police that Emeline was married and that her husband visited periodically. Emeline's mother insisted that her daughter was single.

Aspiring actress Emeline "Dolly" Reynolds. *From the* World, *February 20, 1900.*

The Reynolds family was prosperous. Mr. Reynolds was a Mount Vernon builder who provided well for his family. Emeline moved to Manhattan for a career on the stage. Her dream had not yet been realized, so she sold books, mainly to brokers and bankers. This was how she met "M.B.M.," a New York Stock Exchange broker named Maurice B. Mendham and the man who maid Margaret Adams thought was Emeline's husband.

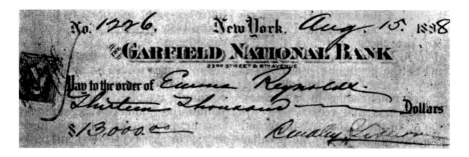

Check endorsed by Dr. Samuel Kennedy that was found hidden in the corset of Emeline Reynolds. *From* The Art of the Handwriting Expert, *1900.*

Police discovered from Emeline's parents that their daughter made a substantial deposit of $500 into the Mount Vernon Bank the previous weekend; thus, they assumed she was doing well financially. Furthermore, Emeline informed her parents she was giving cash to an S.J. Kennedy on the evening of Monday, August 15, so that he could bet it on a horse. Kennedy promised the transaction would net Emeline $4,000. In response, her mother gave her a satchel with a unique screw clasp for storing the money. The satchel was found at the hotel death scene.

Within five hours of discovering the dreadful murder, New York City police arrested Dr. Samuel J. Kennedy, a dentist who resided in New Dorp, Staten Island. Kennedy practiced dentistry at two convenient locations: his New Dorp home and at 60 West Twenty-second Street in Manhattan.

Samuel J. Kennedy was born in Illinois in 1866. When he was two years old, his family moved to New York City, where he was raised and educated in Manhattan. After graduating from the College of the City of New York in 1881, he entered the dental practice of his father, Dr. John C. Kennedy. Two years later, he began studying at the New York College of Dentistry. Graduating at the age of twenty-one, he was the youngest member of his class. After graduation, he entered his father's office as a practicing dentist. The family moved to New Dorp in 1891 and opened a branch of their New York dental rooms. It was claimed that Kennedy was "reckoned by his patients as one of the most careful and skillful dentists on Staten Island." The younger Kennedy had a wife and child and was a popular resident of Rose Avenue, where he shared a house with his parents and their dental practice. An active man, he was a member of the Sea View Tennis and Social Club. Many on Staten Island found it difficult to believe that the well-liked Dr. Kennedy was guilty of murder. Supposedly, he was happy with his

Rising young dentist Dr. Samuel J. Kennedy as he appeared around the age of twenty-six. *From* Prominent Men of Staten Island, *1893.*

marriage. According to the senior Dr. Kennedy, he and his son had eaten breakfast together in their Staten Island home the morning of August 16. The elder Dr. Kennedy implied that his son was in fine spirits.

Dr. Kennedy took his arrest coolly and denied everything except that he knew Emeline Reynolds—and only as a dental patient. Five Grand Hotel employees identified Kennedy as the man with Emeline Reynolds the night she was bludgeoned with the pipe. These included a chambermaid, a bellboy, a headwaiter, a waiter and an elevator boy, thus putting Kennedy at numerous locations within the hotel. For his part, Kennedy denied ever stepping foot into the Grand Hotel. As a matter of fact, he proclaimed that he had no idea where he had been or what he had been doing for the four days previous to his arrest. But he soon "remembered" that he had seen a show at the Proctor Theater the night of Emeline's murder. It had concluded at 11:00 p.m., and Kennedy told the authorities that he was home in New Dorp by 1:00 a.m.

Over time, Kennedy offered additional tidbits to his alibi. He soon stated that after he left his Manhattan office around 5:00 or 6:00 p.m., he went to a furnishing goods store, stopped somewhere for a drink and then returned to his office, where he determined it was high time to put on a newly purchased suit of underwear. He claimed he had fallen asleep for most of the Proctor's performance and thus could not remember one single portion of the presentation, although he did wake up a couple times to hear someone singing. He claimed to be so "dazed" that he slept on the cable car from Twenty-third Street to South Ferry. Aboard the boat to Staten Island, he was again so stupefied that he slept his way across the harbor. When he arrived at the Staten Island terminal, he could not find a lift, so the exhausted Dr. Kennedy walked to New Dorp (a distance of almost six miles). In explaining his dazed condition, Kennedy claimed he was in the habit of using a substance called chloral. In addition, he had dropped a bottle of it on his office floor. It broke, with the result that the fumes went to his head. At this time, chloral was used as a hypnotic-sedative drug, usually in the treatment of insomnia. It was an addictive substance. A therapeutic dose would induce four to eight hours of sleep.

At the precinct where he was being held, Kennedy encountered Maurice Mendham and loudly declared, "You've gotten me into a hell of a lot of trouble."[89] Mendham was a broker who spent much of his time in Long Branch, New Jersey. At the time of the murder, he was staying with his invalid mother at the Hotel Scarboro in that community. A number of people saw him chatting with friends on the porch of the West End Hotel the night Emeline was killed.

Maurice B. Mendham led an interesting and eventful life. Described as handsome and plump, the broker was known for spending money and for his attraction to beautiful young women. It was Mendham who had "installed" Emeline in the West Fifty-eighth Street apartment with the doorplate that read "Mrs. E.C. Reynolds." Before Emeline's death, an odd occurrence took place when she encountered the building's janitress, Mrs. Warnicke, who strongly suggested that Emeline vacate the building because the attention of Mendham was causing a scandal.

Police were surprised that a refined man like Dr. Samuel J. Kennedy would use such a vile weapon. Given his knowledge of anesthetics and poisons, why would he resort to such a battering device? The weapon that killed Emeline Reynolds was a heavy lead pipe. One crooked end provided a usable handle; the other end was wrapped in heavy tape. Why was Emeline Reynolds murdered? One theory suggested that it was because she carried diamonds and jewelry on her person. It was no secret that the stash was kept in a chamois pouch attached to her undergarments. Police believed that at

The mysterious Maurice B. Mendham. *From the* World, *May 16, 1901.*

the time of Emeline's murder, $2,000 worth of diamonds and untold cash were in this pouch. The stones in her earrings alone were valued at $500 each. As for the $13,000 check tucked into Emeline's underclothes, police discovered it was worthless.

After his arraignment on August 17, Samuel J. Kennedy was returned to police headquarters in Manhattan, where he was stripped of his civilian suit for prison attire. It was then that Captain McCluskey observed the new set of drawers worn by the dentist. McCluskey noted that said set of drawers had a telltale mark on the right leg, as did the inside of Kennedy's trousers. McCluskey had sighted a dark, hook-shaped impression in the shape of the lead pipe that had met with Emeline's head. A gummy substance was also found on the inside of the dentist's trousers. It matched the adhesive on the tape wound around the weapon. McCluskey believed Kennedy had attached the bludgeoning device to the interior waistband of his pants so that Emeline could not see it and that, as he moved about, the lead blemished his clothing.

Kennedy claimed that the impressions on his clothing were from the chain that held his keys. But McCluskey reminded Kennedy that he had bought the underwear on Monday and had not borne the keys on his body since that time. So how could the key chain have made the stain? Kennedy was then questioned about the $13,000 check he endorsed. He vehemently denied that it was his signature. At that point, an officer of the Garfield National Bank was brought in with a bank signature card bearing Kennedy's signature for the account he held at this bank. After comparing the signatures, the bank employee stated he would "stake his reputation" on the fact that both signatures were made by the same individual.[90]

McCluskey contended that Kennedy had given Emeline the check to swindle her. Afterward, he returned to the Grand Hotel with the intention of killing her and reclaiming the check so he would not be charged with grand larceny and/or forgery. But after the murder, the much-alarmed Kennedy could not find the check, as he had no idea that Emeline had tucked it to safety in her corset. Kennedy denied the accusation. He also denied that he had stolen her little bag of jewels, which police said included one pair of thirteen-carat solitaire diamond earrings, one diamond star brooch, one turquoise and diamond ring, three rings with Tiffany settings, one diamond ring with two rubies, one ruby ring with two diamonds, one emerald ring with two topazes, one marquise ring of emeralds and diamonds, one large solitaire diamond ring, one little finger ring and one ring with an emerald and diamond cluster. Kennedy was then informed that McCluskey's detectives had found torn scraps of prescription paper from the dentist's office on the hotel fire escape. The words "E. Maxwell and wife" had been written on the paper in Kennedy's hand. McCluskey surmised that the dentist gave it to Reynolds so she would know what name to register under at the Grand Hotel.

In the hunt for evidence, police located salesman Robert Clarke, an employee in the hat department of Smith, Gray & Company. Clarke selected Kennedy out of lineup of eight men, all similar in size and appearance, as the

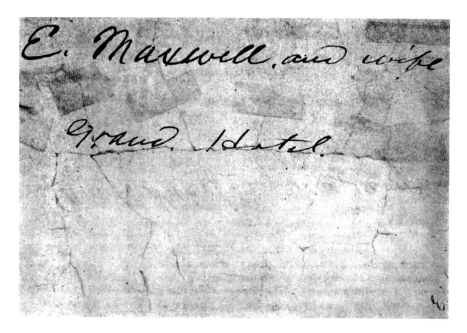

The much disputed and analyzed note bearing the "identity" of the occupants of Room 84 of the Grand Hotel on August 15, 1898. *From* The Art of the Handwriting Expert, *1900.*

customer who had bought a straw hat on August 15. This was important since the five Grand Hotel employees who had identified Kennedy claimed that he wore a straw hat (although detectives were unable to locate the hat when they searched Kennedy's offices and home). Kennedy, when arrested, wore a felt hat, and family, friends and acquaintances insisted that he never owned or wore a straw hat. Kennedy, of course, declared likewise. Clarke actually knew Samuel Kennedy. The salesman had previously sold hats in a Sixth Avenue shop below a dental office run by the elder Kennedy, where Samuel was employed. He recalled this fact when Kennedy bought the straw hat.

At his arraignment, Dr. Kennedy insisted that he had last seen Emeline Reynolds on Friday, August 12. At that time, he claimed to have only "treated her face at his office." Kennedy adamantly maintained that "he never borrowed money from her or had any business transactions with her, that his father was always present when she called at the office, and that he never met Miss Reynolds or any other woman at the Grand Hotel. He absolutely denied all knowledge of the check and said the signature was not his."[91] According to one newspaper, police were working on the theory that Kennedy was part of a wiretapping gang. Simply put, these hoodlums "pretended to tap wires leading to poolrooms for the purpose of intercepting news of horse races."[92] The gang then held back the reports until they could wager on the winner in the poolroom. Kennedy's part was to find "lambs," people who were willing to hand over money to bet. Meanwhile, the so-called wiretappers did not tap anything, but the lamb believed they did. When the lamb demanded his money, the gang scared the lamb away by saying police were on to the scheme and they had to leave town quickly. They, of course, "departed" with the lamb's money. Along these lines, the $13,000 check found on Emeline was the "windfall" Kennedy promised if she invested in the horse racing scheme. But there was no profit, and the check held no value, so Kennedy killed her.[93]

At the coroner's inquiry, all eyes strained to see the tiny, pale woman clad in black who took the stand. In a low voice with a slight German accent, Emeline's mother, Mrs. Cristina Reynolds, reiterated that her daughter was to meet with Dr. Kennedy at 6:00 p.m. on Monday, August 15, to receive the winnings from her investment.

As was often the case when an independent woman was wronged, the media began judging the victim. The *Evening Press* went so far as to write, "Emeline unquestionably was a bad girl. One man says: 'I could name seventy-five Wall St. men besides Maurice Mendham who knew her. Maury was putting up the money.' She was a monomaniac on the subject of money."[94] (Note the slanderous use of the word "knew.")

Regarding the missing jewels, the police department announced on August 25 that they were not missing at all. A servant discovered them behind a sugar can in Emeline's apartment.

The murder trial of Emeline Reynolds began on March 21, 1899. At trial, defendant Dr. Samuel Kennedy was as carefree as a flitting butterfly in summer. His aged, white-haired father and loyal wife remained steadfast in their belief that Kennedy was innocent, as did his father-in-law, Samuel Eaton Sr., who was also in court.

Grand Hotel staff soon took the stand. They verified that Kennedy was indeed the man observed in the presence of Miss Reynolds on August 15. He was the man in the room when the bottle of champagne was delivered. He was the man who departed the hotel around 2:00 a.m. on August 16. Surprising new evidence came from Mrs. W.S. Logue of Baltimore, Maryland, who was in Room 52 of the Grand Hotel the night Emeline Reynolds was slaughtered. Her third-floor accommodation was directly below the murder room. Mrs. Logue informed the court that on the night of

Emeline's death, she heard people walking above her. She was memorably startled by the unexpected fall of a heavy object hitting the floor. Another thud on the floor was followed by the sound of solitary footsteps. Soon all noise ceased, and she fell asleep. On cross-examination, Mrs. Logue swore that she was not mistaken about hearing the sounds.

Chemist Ernest J. Lederle of the health board next took the stand. In discussing the murder weapon, Lederle displayed an iron rod running through a length of lead pipe, which he said was identical to similar metal found in Kennedy's Staten Island home.

Handwriting expert William Kinsley verified that the torn prescription slip with the words "E. Maxwell and wife" found in bits on the fire escape was written by the same hand that wrote out the $13,000 check. Two additional handwriting experts, Daniel T. Ames and William E. Hagan, verified Kinsley's conclusion.

Kennedy's defense countered with the elder Dr. John Kennedy stating that neither the check nor the slip of paper was written by his son. He insisted that Samuel was with him in their Manhattan office until 4:00 p.m. on the day of Emeline's murder, after which the younger man went to the theater. The father swore that he did not see his son again until 7:30 a.m. the following morning, when they had breakfast together at their New Dorp home. Samuel Eaton Sr. testified that he saw the younger Kennedy on August 15 and was told that he was going to Proctors Theater to see a show. Next to take the stand was William Ufer, who described meeting Kennedy at the corner of Sixth Avenue and Twenty-eighth Street, where at 7:30 p.m., they shook hands and the dentist informed him he was on his way to the theater. Additional questioning brought forth the fact that Ufer was a regular visitor of Kennedy while he was being held in the Tombs prison awaiting trial. In addition, Ufer worked for a man named Simpson. A check made out to Simpson from Kennedy for $550 was presented at the trial. When asked why the payment was made to Simpson, Ufer replied that he had no idea.

The defense opened its case with six individuals who stated that Dr. Samuel Kennedy had an excellent reputation. One of the individuals called to the stand was Richmond County borough president George Cromwell.

Many on Staten Island were shocked when Dr. Samuel J. Kennedy was convicted of murdering Emeline "Dolly" Reynolds and was sentenced to die in the electric chair of Sing Sing Prison during the week of May 22, 1899. The killer took the verdict calmly. When asked by Judge Williams if he wanted to make a statement, Kennedy stated that yes, he did. He insisted his conviction resulted from perjurers hired or threatened by the New York

Staten Island borough president George Cromwell was an avid believer in Dr. Kennedy's innocence. *From* Morris's Memorial History of Staten Island, *1900.*

City Police Department. He stated, "My conscience is perfectly clear, and perfectly clean, and I have nothing to reproach myself for in respect to the Dolly Reynolds murder."[95] On March 31, after removal from Murderer's Row at the Tombs prison in Manhattan, Kennedy was caged at the Sing Sing Prison Death House.

An extremely odd message arrived in New York from "across the pond" in May 1899. Convict Richard T. Nicholson, incarcerated at the descriptive-sounding Wormwood Scrubs in London, England, claimed responsibility for killing Emeline Reynolds. Nicholson swore he was a former member of the Seventy-first Regiment who had served in Cuba. Afterward, he met Emeline in New York, where the two went to a hotel and became "intimate." At the hotel, a vicious quarrel ensued, with him shooting Emeline and then fleeing. But Nicholson was missing one important detail: Reynolds had been beaten to death, not shot. British authorities sent the confession to Governor Theodore Roosevelt, who forwarded it to New York City officials for investigation. Police called Nicholson a "plain, unvarnished liar." They believed he was hoping to get a free ride to America when his imprisonment concluded the following year. Friend & House, counsel to Dr. Kennedy, placed great faith in the Nicholson confession.

By the end of 1899, Kennedy's conviction was before the court of appeals. Many Staten Island residents were pleased. His bowling club even organized a fundraiser to gather "a purse to engage counsel" in the hope that a new trial would be announced. It was believed that former Richmond County district attorney Sidney F. Rawson of De Groot, Rawson and Strafford of Port Richmond would argue the case. Steadfastly declaring Kennedy's innocence, Dr. T.S. Yocum, pastor of Saint Andrew's Episcopal Church, was instrumental in getting financial backers for the bowling extravaganza.

Dr. Kennedy was introduced to a new "neighbor" at Sing Sing Prison on February 16, 1900, when Roland B. Molineux arrived for incarceration. Molineux had been convicted of murder in the first degree for poisoning Katherine Adams after a media headlining trial. While Molineux readied himself for breakfast with his first prison sponge bath, Kennedy whistled a jolly tune. Interestingly, Dr. Kennedy had a prison house reputation for his jovial moods and activities. Kennedy's cell was closest to Molineux, so the newcomer shouted out, "Good morning, friend. You seem happy."[96] Kennedy responded that he was not particularly cheerful but that he saw no use in complaining. They chatted back and forth, with Molineux asking about prison meals, to which Kennedy replied it was all that could be desired. Special convicts were allowed to receive food from loved ones after it had been inspected by prison staff; hence, Molineux was expected to receive fodder via family.

Citing errors made at Dr. Kennedy's trial, the New York State Court of Appeals called for a new trial on November 20, 1900. Justice Haight made particular note of Detective Price's evidence, which he wrote "was more from hearsay than from material, and was also incompetent and prejudicial to the defendant."[97] When the retrial was announced, Emeline's parents were astonished. Mrs. Reynolds acknowledged that Kennedy was guilty but claimed that another man was much more to blame for her daughter's demise. In fact, she blamed Wall Street executive Maurice B. Mendham. According to Mrs. Reynolds, at the time of the murder, Emeline was engaged to Mendham, who had put the wedding off several times. Mendham convinced Emeline that he was a well-off southern gentleman. Mrs. Reynolds believed that Dr. Kennedy was the broker's "tool" and that Mendham had supplied funding for more experienced lawyers to file an appeal.

Dr. Samuel J. Kennedy stood before the Supreme Court in Manhattan for commencement of his second trial in the murder of Emeline Reynolds on February 4, 1901. Smiling and stepping briskly into the courtroom, Kennedy's father was again present to support him. William Cantwell and Robert Moore were enlisted to defend the convicted murderer. Rumors circulated that an unnamed man would come forward and state that he was the man who had been with Emeline the night before her murder. So brave was this mystery man that he would present this information even though it could cost him his own reputation. Even so, he would do the right thing since he was not the murderer. This man of clarity never materialized. In addition, the new lawyers asserted that a provable alibi for Kennedy's whereabouts on the night of the murder would be provided.

Prosecutor Forbes J. Hennessey opened the case before Justice Edgar L. Fursman on February 7, 1901. Hennessey began with the ridiculous sentiment that everyone knew Dolly Reynolds "was not a good girl," but even so, "her life was as valuable before the law as that of the highest woman."[98] Employees of the Grand Hotel once again verified that Dr. Samuel J. Kennedy was present at the hotel the night of the murder. One issue encountered by the defense was the absence of star witness Daniel Melville, who had unexpectedly departed on a steamer ship for a honeymoon trip to Florida (the plumber later said doctors advised him the trip was necessary for his wife's health). The defense contended that Melville would substantiate that the pipe presented by police at the first trial was not from Kennedy's home. Instead, it had been removed from Melville's place of business by police to frame Kennedy. Originally, the pipe was said to be from Kennedy's Staten Island residence, and it supposedly corresponded to the pipe used in the weapon that killed Emeline.

On February 13, all were stunned when chemist Dr. Ernest Lederle contradicted his original testimony that the pipe in the weapon and the pipe allegedly found by police in the Kennedy home were the same. He now claimed the diameter of each was different, as was the appearance. Kennedy and his wife, who sat together in the courtroom, were visibly delighted, while the jury was notably surprised.

As the trial progressed, Dr. Kennedy was said by one newspaper to be admirably composed—even the most damaging evidence did not cause the dentist to "quiver." According to the tabloid, "it gives him credit for more strength of character than one would suspect from his effeminate makeup."[99]

The prosecution was handed an unexpected blow when Judge Fursman excluded the expertise of a handwriting analyst who would testify that it

Dr. Samuel J. Kennedy strides into the courtroom for his second trial in the murder of Emeline Reynolds. *From the* World, *February 11, 1901.*

Dr. and Mrs. Samuel J. Kennedy were confident that the dentist would be acquitted at his second trial. *From the* World, *February 5, 1901.*

was Dr. Kennedy who wrote the check found on Emeline's body, as well as the "E. Maxwell and wife" note. The judge said both "were only bits of evidence, and bits of evidence cannot be compared for the purpose of establishing handwriting" when the handwriting expert is not thoroughly familiar with the writing of the defendant.[100]

Dr. Kennedy wrote an emotional plea proclaiming his innocence, which was published in the *World* newspaper on February 15, 1901. Saying that he had refrained from writing such on the advice of his counsel, Kennedy proclaimed that he was "elated" that the court case had turned in his favor. He was now confident of acquittal.

Attorney Cantwell kicked off the defense by proclaiming, "This crime was never committed by this man. It was too brutal, too horrible to have

By the turn of the century, the *World* showcased crimes with stunning drawings and depictions. *From* King's Handbook of New York City, *1892*.

been committed by a man of his refinement and education."[101] Cantwell swore that Kennedy was not in the Grand Hotel the night Emeline was bludgeoned to death. He stated that nine people saw Kennedy the night of the murder—away from the Grand Hotel. One who could verify this claim was a Mrs. Slaytor, who had died, but her statement at the previous trial would be read in court. Cantwell inferred that Emeline was often beaten by a man who supported her financially, adding that a witness who had heard this man tell her "I will see you in Hell someday" would be brought into the courtroom.[102]

Samuel Kennedy's mother took the stand, and all were brought to tears as she validated her son's alibi on the night of Emeline Reynolds's murder. According to the *World*, "It was the most pathetic and dramatic scene of the trial, and the spectacle of the infirm, gray haired woman on the stand aiding in establishing the alibi upon which her son's life depends was one to be long remembered."[103] It was even written that Dr. Kennedy's tears mingled with hers as they embraced after her testimony. On the same day, plumber Melville made his first appearance in court, where he was sharply rebuked for leaving town after a subpoena had been issued for his appearance. Fursman ordered him held in custody until the morning. That would give him plenty of time to explain to the judge why he shouldn't be punished for contempt. Again, Kennedy's good reputation was attested to by Staten Island borough president Cromwell. In addition, the defense brought in millionaire real estate owner and manufacturer David Tysen and Reverend Dr. Thomas Yocum of Saint Andrew's Church, who continued to be adamant that Kennedy was innocent.

For his unscheduled departure to Florida, Melville was fined twenty-five dollars. This was half the fifty-dollar fine Justice Fursman wanted to impose. It appears the judge was sympathetic to the plumber's plight in removing his wife to warmer climes due to her declining health.

Locked up for over twenty-three hours, the jurors in the second trial of Dr. Samuel Kennedy could not agree on a verdict. With that, they were officially released from service by Justice Fursman on February 22, 1901. It was believed that the jurymen initially stood eleven to one for acquittal. In the end, seven voted for conviction, five against. Appearing haggard after the ordeal, the twelve men entered the courtroom. Jury foreman James Klaber held out for conviction and stated emphatically that he refused to change his mind. Kennedy's eyes never left Klaber's face, even as the foreman exited the courtroom. Kennedy then turned to his father and said, "I am greatly disappointed." With that, Kennedy was escorted to the court

Reverend T. Yocum of the Church of Saint Andrew's worked diligently to raise funds for Kennedy's second trial. *From* History of Richmond County, Staten Island, *1887.*

pen by the sheriff. Mrs. Kennedy responded, "We will yet have you back home again, and I for one will never forsake you."[104] Prosecutors swore that Kennedy would be tried again. Mrs. Kennedy bemoaned that she knew not where additional trial money would be found. But she was assured by John Purcell, chairman of the committee that had previously raised $2,000 for Kennedy's defense, that Staten Islanders would again rally around her man and contribute the necessary funds. Shortly after the second trial, it came to light that Mrs. Kennedy's father, Samuel Eaton, was an astrologer and had predicted this experience for Kennedy years ago. Too bad he had not informed them of the need to establish a fund for this future dilemma.

The third trial against Dr. Samuel J. Kennedy was initiated on May 6, 1901. Unlike in the previous trials, Mrs. Kennedy was not allowed to sit alongside her husband, the court believing that too much sympathy resulted from this seating arrangement. As often occurred in third trials, it became difficult to select jurors without knowledge of the murder (and why would you want anyone not following current events?) or who would allow themselves to be involved in such prominent proceedings. As headlining court cases, the Kennedy trials, like other sensational trials, attracted their share of odd individuals making outlandish claims.

On May 11, 1901, Mrs. Edith Heathmere and her sixteen-year-old daughter, Lillian, arrived at the courthouse to speak to Magistrate Brann. Carrying an oversized satchel, Mrs. Heathmere extracted a dazzling array of papers, which she advised the court were relevant to the murder of Emeline Reynolds. Furthermore, Mrs. Heathmere claimed that she and her child were residents of the Grand Hotel when the slaughter of Miss Reynolds took place. She further advised Magistrate Brann that the $13,000 check tucked into Emeline Reynolds's bodice was, in fact, her property and that police had stolen it from her to bolster their case against Dr. Kennedy. Brann listened quietly and politely until Mrs. Heathmere completed her complaint. When she was finished, he called to the clerk of the court and whispered that he should immediately draw up the necessary paperwork to commit both mother and daughter to the insane pavilion at Bellevue Hospital. Very cooperative individuals, the Heathmeres were carted off, without protest or annoyance, in an enclosed carriage to the facility, where their rationality would be investigated. A Dr. Wildman (an interesting name for a doctor at such an institution) declared they were suffering from "nervous prostration," exacerbated by the belief that they were victims of a conspiracy. Both women were well known at the courthouse, as they had attended every session of both Kennedy trials. On more than one occasion, they had informed the district attorney that yes, Dr. Kennedy was being tried on "manufactured evidence." It would later come to light that Mrs. Heathmere authored a lengthy letter in which she thoroughly outlined why, in her opinion, Dr. Kennedy was innocent. This letter was mailed to one of the jurors during the progress of the trial. Known to be very well off, Mrs. Heathmere often paid her bills in gold. But no matter what they believed, Mrs. Heathmere and Lillian were always courteous and quiet. Doctors proclaimed both women mentally unbalanced and called for their placement in a private sanitarium. Eventually, a court order called for their release, so they were placed under the care of a friend. Doctors did not fight the decision. While mother and daughter might have been mad, all knew they were harmless.

In his opening speech, Assistant District Attorney O'Connor stated, "Oh Lord, Oh Lord, throw light upon this straw hat that we may find out whether this defendant is guilty or innocent. Never shall the people be satisfied until we find out what has become of this straw hat. We shall cry out straw hat until the day of judgment or until this straw hat has been found. We shall erase the word innocent stamped on his brow and place instead the flaming letters of guilty!"[105] In response, defense attorney Moore said, "This is not an opening address," to which Judge Newberger responded, "Objection sustained." It was a poor opening "statement" that the prosecution presented.

At this, the third trial of Dr. Samuel Kennedy, broker Maurice Mendham finally appeared before the court. Oddly enough, he had not been previously called. To some, he was a mythical figure in Miss Reynolds's life. He was referred to but never mentioned by name. The prosecution planned to display Mendham so the jury would believe Kennedy had a motive for killing Emeline.

On the afternoon of May 16, Maurice Mendham took the stand. Referred to as a "recalcitrant witness," he appeared deeply troubled. "He balked at questions" and "refused to answer some on the grounds that they would tend to degrade him."[106] Mendham flatly refused to verify that he and Miss Reynolds lived together as husband and wife. When Judge Newberger asked why he would not answer the question, Mendham replied, "It might reflect upon the dead woman." When asked where he was the night of Emeline's murder, Mendham responded that he was in Long Branch, New Jersey. He further informed the court that he had known Dr. Kennedy for fifteen years and that, yes, he had introduced him to Emeline. When asked where Emeline carried her little bag of jewels, Mendham replied, "About the waist." When asked if he had seen the bag about her waist, he replied that he did not care to answer. After further questioning, he said he saw it about her corset. When questioned by the defense, Mendham acknowledged that some believed he was Mr. Reynolds and that, yes, they did live together as man and wife. Robert Moore asked Mendham if he knew a young woman named Cozzens who died mysteriously in 1893 while living with Mendham. This so enraged Mendham that he half sprang out of the chair and yelled, "I would like to cross examine you if I had a chance."[107]

All were perplexed when it was revealed that Mendham had sent Emeline Reynolds a telegram on Tuesday, August 16, 1898—hours after he was informed that she was dead. What was the reason behind sending the telegram? His response: "I wanted to account for [my] absence on Monday."[108]

This third trial was characterized by numerous statements that contradicted testimony from the first two trials. Time and again, witnesses changed their earlier testimony, especially in the case of the Grand Hotel employees who first identified Kennedy as the man with Emeline Reynolds on the night of the murder. Now, they were not positive that Kennedy was the man. At this trial, handwriting analysis was allowed. Garfield National Bank teller George D. Weekes stated his belief that the body of the check "was in the characteristic handwriting of Dr. Kennedy." Judge Newberger also allowed the jury to see photographs of Kennedy's signature, as well as the original "E. Maxwell and wife" note that had been ripped up. It was now acknowledged that the note was written on the back of a Philips Milk of Magnesia prescription blank. Defense attorney Moore quickly objected to jurors viewing this evidence. After explaining his concerns to Newberger, the judge had the handwriting examples taken from the jury. Said to be a "wizard" at handwriting identification, John F. Tyrell was called to the stand. He informed all that he believed the check, the check endorsement and the "E. Maxwell and wife" note were all written by the same person, Dr. Samuel J. Kennedy. The prosecution went on to present four more experts, who agreed that the three examples of evidence were written by Dr. Kennedy. In turn, the defense produced an assortment of experts who stated that Kennedy did not write the note, check or the endorsement. Instead, they asserted, they were forgeries meant to replicate Kennedy's handwriting.

Milliner Annie Melville, who worked in a shop below Kennedy's dental office on West Twenty-second Street, was put on the stand. Said to be "white as a sheet" in fear of being cross-examined by Assistant District Attorney Osborne, Mrs. Melville had not testified at the previous trials. Brought on as a witness for the defense, she swore that she saw Kennedy leave his office between 5:00 and 5:30 p.m. on the day of the murder. Furthermore, she said he wore a dark derby, which she believed was black. Mrs. Melville also claimed that on that same day, a man who was taller and heavier than Dr. Kennedy came in the store. The mystery man had a similar mustache and a straw hat. This man had also been in the shop about ten days earlier, asking questions about the dentist. With that, Robert Moore ceased asking questions, and Mr. Osborne declined to cross-examine the witness. No reason was given as to why the woman had not reported this information earlier. The defense went on to bring additional witnesses to provide Kennedy with an alibi. Franklin Roberts swore he saw Kennedy on the 12:55 a.m. Staten Island–bound ferryboat and that Kennedy was drunk and walked into him. This was Roberts's first appearance at a Kennedy trial as well. Cab driver Alfred Wagner swore he saw an intoxicated Kennedy staggering off the 12:55 a.m. boat with his black derby sideways on his head.

Robert Moore emphatically charged the "police with conspiring to railroad his client on patched-up evidence."[109] He stated that the pipe was a puzzling piece of proof. It was not found on the first search of Kennedy's home. It was not found until police went to Melville's shop, after which the plumber discovered a similar piece missing. Both the prosecution and the defense charged that witnesses had been tampered with and that conspiracy

Emeline Reynolds's sister Helen, as depicted by the *World* on May 31, 1901. Journalists were quick to note that the siblings were beautiful.

theories abounded. At the trial's end, men and women jostled one another for entrance to the courtroom. "Every seat was occupied in a twinkling," even though they were earmarked for individuals connected to the case.

According to the *World*, Mr. Osborne's presentation of the state's case "was one of the most powerful arraignments ever heard in the criminal courts of New York." The prosecutor dissected and disavowed many of the plausible defense theories. "In the opinion of many of the spectators, the jurors were powerfully affected." At the close of Osborne's summation, Mrs.

District Attorney James W. Osborne presents his closing argument at Dr. Kennedy's third trial. *From the* World, *June 14, 1901.*

Kennedy commented, "I have only one thing to look forward to, and that is the acquittal of my husband."[110]

At 12:20 p.m. on Saturday, June 15, 1901, Justice Newberger gave the case over to the twelve men of the jury. Newberger was "exceptionally powerful and unprejudiced" in his charge to the jurors. The judge was adamant that if the jurors found that Kennedy killed Emeline Reynolds in a state of "voluntary intoxication," they must find him guilty in the first degree. "If the intoxication was not voluntary, and if it was such that it rendered Kennedy unable to form a definite intent to kill, then they might find him guilty in the second degree."[111]

As the jury left for lunch at the Astor House, gawkers shouted "Let him loose! Let him go!" thus signaling the crowd's sympathies. At 5:00 p.m., it was reported that eight stood in favor of acquitting Kennedy, while four determined that he belonged back at Sing Sing's Murderer's Row for electrocution. After ten hours and forty minutes, the jury could not reach a decision. It was 11:00 p.m., so they were locked up for the night. They were informed that if they did not reach a decision by 10:30 a.m. the following morning, they would be dismissed. The only communication received from the jury was that juror Farnes wanted the cigars in his suitcase. All took this as a sign that a deadlock had occurred and that it was a "case of siege."

Mrs. Kennedy, her parents and Dr. Kennedy's parents departed the courthouse for a car to take them to South Ferry. As they left, a crowd gathered behind and followed their steps. As the swarm grew, their silence intensified, but when the party boarded the car for the terminal, the crowd let loose with, "You'll have him all-right to-morrow. Hurrah for Mr. Moore! Hurrah for Dr. Kennedy!"[112]

After a 7:30 a.m. breakfast, the jury began deliberating again, but it was no use. Judge Newberger ascended the bench at 10:15 a.m. The jury was brought in, as was the defendant. When asked by the judge if it were true that the jury was unable to reach a verdict, the foreman announced that yes, it was true. "For a second Dr. Kennedy seemed unable to comprehend. Then the tears came to his eyes."[113] Newberger released the jury and remanded the defendant. One of the points that the jurors could not agree on was the identification of Kennedy as the individual who departed the Grand Hotel early in the morning of August 16, 1898. They did not believe it was reliable, as the witness had only a side or back view. Since two jurors were unable to convict Kennedy, and because all were aware that there would not be a fourth trial, Robert Moore stated that two disagreements equaled an acquittal. In response, Assistant District Attorney Osborne stated sadly, "It is a triumph of murder—a triumph of fraud and chicanery…there is more than a suspicion when witnesses drop from the clouds at a period of three years after the murder."[114] Osborne was not the only one displeased. The public was quite disgusted that the three trials had cost the city of New York a whopping $112,000, with much of that attributed to paying for scientific and handwriting experts.

On June 18, torpedo inventor Lieutenant E.E. Hand of the U.S. Navy went before bond clerk Pierce Poole to offer security for Dr. Samuel J. Kennedy's bail. Upon inspection, it was found that the apartment house he offered was in the name of his wife, Eleanor, and that an unrecorded mortgage was held on the property. As such, the lieutenant brought his wife in to secure the bail, and Kennedy was released.

"Samuel J. Kennedy, dentist, went in a sort of triumphal procession yesterday to his home at New Dorp, Staten Island after an absence of nearly three years, twenty one months of which were spent in the death house of Sing Sing," wrote the *Sun* on June 19, 1901.[115] When the deputy sheriff removed him from Murderer's Row at the Tombs, Kennedy shook hands with the prisoners as they shouted, "Three cheers for Dr. Kennedy." As Kennedy made his victorious walk to Moore's law office, a crowd of spectators, reporters and photographers thronged alongside them. The cheering mob swelled so much that electric cars, drays and cabs were blockaded. At Moore's office, Kennedy was introduced to two more witnesses who, need be, would testify that they knew the identity of Kennedy's double—the man who actually killed Emeline Reynolds. They claimed that Miss Reynolds rented a secret room from them that she seldom used. According to these unnamed witnesses, the double appeared, picked up a letter addressed to Miss Reynolds under the name Mrs. E. Maxwell and vanished. When they saw Kennedy, they supposedly swore that he was not the man who picked up the letter. When Kennedy and Moore finally reached South Ferry, they boarded the *Robert Garrett*. Captain Cole invited them into the pilothouse, where Kennedy complained that all of the sunlight irritated his eyes, as he was unaccustomed to such brightness. At his New Dorp residence, Kennedy declared that he had not killed Emeline Reynolds and that the district attorney should do all in his power to find the real culprit. Shortly after 8:00 p.m., the Kennedys went to a nearby hotel for a light meal. Along their walking route, electric lights and Chinese lanterns festooned the trees in celebration of his release and return to Staten Island. Approximately two thousand individuals were said to be at the hotel upon his arrival. Fireworks were even set off to celebrate the acquittal.

Mrs. Kennedy vowed that her dentist husband would practice again—solely on Staten Island. Mrs. Kennedy firmly asserted, "I would never be satisfied to have him open an office in New-York again."[116]

Six months after the acquittal of her son, the "ailing, fragile" Mrs. Marion Kennedy headed to Pittsburgh. Claiming to be the nearest living relative of her bachelor cousin John Charles, who died a very wealthy man, she was going west to present a claim—she wanted the majority share of Mr. Charles's $100,000 estate, so she hired the law office of Mr. Robert Moore to get it. It was Mr. Moore's opinion that she was not a second cousin; indeed, he said the good Mrs. Kennedy was a first cousin.

On November 26, 1901, Robert Moore questioned the district attorney of Manhattan about a rumor that Dr. Samuel Kennedy was being retried for the murder of Emeline Reynolds. The DA responded that it was not true. Moore noted that the Kennedys had enlarged their New Dorp home and that the Staten Island dental office was flourishing. No doubt lawyer Moore's practice was also flourishing.

The mysterious Maurice Mendham died in November 1912. His presence in Emeline Reynolds's life was never fully explained beyond a hint that he was something of a "sugar daddy." It is surprising that more suspicion was not cast upon the man since Dr. Kennedy was acquitted and in light of the ambiguity that encircled the death of Alice Cozzens, especially after his shocking marriage to twenty-two-year-old Francis Cartwright when he was fifty-five. What really raised the eyebrows of already high-browed New Yorkers was that the girl had been his legal ward since the age of fifteen.

Beautiful, young and vibrant Alice Cozzens was hoping for a successful career in the exciting world of New York City entertainment. Instead, she was found dead in the Coleman House in Manhattan on the morning of March 12, 1893. About eighteen years old, Alice had checked in as Mrs. F. Carter of St. Louis at 11:00 p.m. the previous evening. Coroner Messemer performed an autopsy and found that she had died from a bullet wound to the heart. She was not a drug addict, but there was laudanum and probably milk punch in her stomach. "The autopsy, while not revealing that the young woman had the dread of maternity as an incentive to suicide, suggested that she might have been driven to the deed by remorse for recent conduct and had a reason for passing herself, in contemplation of suicide, as a married woman."[117] The publications of the day were quick to note that while her outward clothing was intact, she lacked undergarments. Since none were found in the room, it was assumed she checked in without any. Maurice Mendham's name circulated with that of Cozzen's suicide. In fact, the young

Top: An early protégé of Maurice Mendham's, Alice Cozzens committed suicide in March 1893. *From the* National Police Gazette, *April 1, 1893.*

Left: The *National Police Gazette* of April 1, 1893, showing its version of the "Alice Cozzens Mysterious Suicide," including a possible murderer departing via a Coleman House window.

girl had told her parents she might visit Mendham the evening she checked into the Coleman House. Mendham was known for his pleasure-seeking habits and for the attention he gave to pretty young women. According to one friend, "A new face, if a handsome one, appealed to him strongly."[118] Initially, Mendham said he only knew the girl casually. Then he claimed they met only about fifteen times or so. Still later, he divulged that he suggested she submit a play to him so he could review it, which he did. As such, some called her his protégé.

The indictment against Kennedy was eventually dropped, and no one was ever convicted for the brutal slaughter of Emeline Reynolds. Owing to the notoriety of Room 84, many guests refused the quarters where Emeline "Dolly" Reynolds was bludgeoned that summer day. As such, Grand Hotel management changed its number—business was business, synchronized numbers be damned. The Grand Hotel building still stands but is today an apartment house. It is not nearly as grand or mysterious as it once was, unlike the murder of Emeline Reynolds, which, to this day, remains unsolved.

NOTES

INTRODUCTION

1. Scott, "A Murder on Staten Island in 1744."
2. Ibid.

CHAPTER 1

3. *New York Herald*, "$200 Reward."
4. Ibid., "$500 Reward."
5. Ibid., "City Intelligence."
6. *Evening Express*, "The Staten Island Mystery—Again."
7. Ibid., "Local Intelligence."
8. Ibid.
9. *Evening Star*, April 7, 1859.
10. *Belmont Chronicle*, "The Brennan [*sic*] Mystery."
11. Ibid.
12. Ibid.
13. *Evening Express*, "The Brannan Divorce Case."
14. Ibid.
15. *Daily National Republican*, "The Brannan Divorce Case."

CHAPTER 2

16. *New York Tribune,* "Murder."
17. Ibid.
18. Ibid.
19. *Albany Argus*, "Death of a Murderer."
20. Ibid.

CHAPTER 3

21. *New York Times,* "A Fatal Sword Thrust."
22. Ibid.
23. Ibid.
24. Ibid.
25. Ibid., "Was It a Duel?"
26. Ibid.
27. *Brooklyn Eagle*, "He Was Killed in a Duel."
28. *New York Times,* "Fatally Stabbed."
29. *Evening World,* "Still a Mystery."
30. Ibid.,"It Is the Mafia Now."

CHAPTER 4

31. Shepherd, *Sailors' Snug Harbor.*
32. Ibid.
33. Ibid.
34. *New York Times*, "Murder and Suicide on Staten Island."
35. *Evening Express*, "Staten Island."

CHAPTER 5

36. *New York Times*, "Death After a Brawl."
37. Ibid.
38. Ibid.
39. *Daily Graphic*, "The Killing of Edward Drury."

CHAPTER 6

40. *New York Times*, "Straight Edgers' Society."
41. *Sun*, "The Straight Edge People."
42. Ibid., "Apply the Golden Rule."
43. Ibid.; *New York Times*, "Straight Edgers' Society."
44. *New York Times*, "Straight Edgers' Society."
45. *Sun*, "Straight Edge Life Hard."
46. Ibid., "The Straight Edge People."
47. Ibid., "Was Straight Edger; in Jail."
48. Ibid.
49. *World*, "Fell Dead at Minister's Murder Trial."
50. *New York Press*, "Old Man Drops Dead at Murder Trial."
51. *World*, "Minister Guilty of Manslaughter."

CHAPTER 7

52. *Union-Sun and Journal*, "Two Women Slain in a Lonely Spot on Staten Island"; *Brooklyn Daily Eagle*, "2 Girls Found Slain, Brutally Cut Bodies Hurled Out of Auto"; *Daily Argus*, "Two Slain Women Tossed from Auto on Staten Island Road."
53. *New York Times*, "Two Women Slain; Suspect Gang Plot."
54. *Utica Observer-Dispatch*, "Salerno Girl Had Divorced One Husband."
55. Ibid., "Never Happy But Always Smiling Was Elvira Salerno, Murdered."

56. *Brooklyn Daily Eagle*, "Two Arraigned in Staten Island Double Murder."
57. *New York Times*, "Three Men Sought for Slaying Women."
58. *Brooklyn Daily Eagle*, "Two Arraigned in Staten Island Double Murder."
59. *Brooklyn Standard Union*, "Startling Turn Expected in Dual Slasher Murder."
60. Ibid.
61. *Evening Telegram*, "Believe Auto Used in Dual Slaying Is Found."
62. *New York Times*, "Three Men Sought for Slaying Women."
63. *Brooklyn Standard Union*, "Wrong Identification of One Victim Adds to Mystery of Murders."
64. *Daily Sentinel*, "Blandino Woman Friend of Ponzi"; *Utica Observer-Dispatch*, "Di Pasquale Sought by Police Probing Murder of Women."
65. *New York Times*, "Staten Island Clue to Girl Slayers"; *Utica Observer-Dispatch*, "Di Pasquale Sought by Police Probing Murder of Women."
66. *New York Times*, "Boy Finds Body of Murdered Man."

CHAPTER 8

67. *Evening World*, "Six Men Indicted, Four for Murder, in Bootleg Slaying."
68. *Evening Telegram*, "To Bare Rum Ring at Murder Trail."
69. Ibid.
70. *Evening World*, "Jurors 'Get Air' in Autos to be Fit for Murder Trial."
71. *Evening Telegram*, "Dramatic End in Murder Trial."
72. *New York Tribune*, "Betray Slayers or Risk Death, Court Tells Man."
73. *New York Call*, "High Brow Death House Champ."
74. *Evening Telegram*, "Least Coveted Title."
75. *New York Times*, "Death House to Freedom."

CHAPTER 9

76. Reycraft, "1920—West Brighton Strangling."
77. *New York Times*, "Identify Woman Slain in Thicket."
78. *New York Tribune*, "Slain Woman Is Identified by Husband."

79. *New York Times*, "Identify Woman Slain in Thicket"; *Standard Union*, "Husband Identifies Victim of Strangler"; Reycraft, "1920—West Brighton Strangling."
80. Ibid.

CHAPTER 10

81. *Brooklyn Daily Eagle*, "First Lunacy Trial Is Held Before U.S. Court Here."
82. *New York Times*, "Soldier Killer Held Insane."

CHAPTER 11

83. Mogelever, "Our Unsolved Murders: Body Found in Woods."

CHAPTER 12

84. *New York Times*, "Woman Murdered in Hotel."
85. *Brooklyn Eagle*, "Found Dead in a Hotel."
86. *New York Times*, "Woman Murdered in Hotel."
87. *New York Herald*, "Murder Ends Her Hotel Romance."
88. *Brooklyn Eagle*, "Found Dead in a Hotel."
89. *New York Times*, "Woman Murdered in Hotel."
90. *Sun*, "Did Kennedy Murder Her?"
91. *New York Times*, "Reynolds Murder Case."
92. *Sun*, "Sure Kennedy Killed Her."
93. Ibid.
94. *Evening Press*, "On the Tip of the Tongue."

95. *New York Times*, "Kennedy Sentenced to Die."
96. *New York Tribune*, "Molineux Is Cheerful."
97. Ibid., "New Trial for Kennedy."
98. Ibid., "Kennedy Trial Fairly Begun."
99. *World*, "Bludgeon Evidence for Dr. Kennedy."
100. Ibid., "Kennedy Decision May Free Molineux."
101. Ibid., "Four Witnesses Saw Kennedy on Fatal Day."
102. Ibid.
103. Ibid., "Kennedy's Judge Gets Anonymous Letters."
104. Ibid., "Kennedy Jury Disagrees."
105. *Sun*, "Kennedy Jury Completed."
106. *World*, "Broker Mendham Tells of Dolly Reynolds's Life."
107. Ibid.
108. *New York Tribune*, "Good Day for Kennedy."
109. *World*, "Kennedy Is Victim of Plot."
110. Ibid., "Dr. Kennedy Fiercely Arraigned, Now Awaits Judge's Last Word."
111. *World*, "Eight to Four for Kennedy."
112. *Sun*, "Kennedy Jury Is Split."
113. *Buffalo Evening Express*, "Kennedy Jury Fails to Reach an Agreement."
114. *World*, "Delay in the Kennedy Case."
115. *Sun*, "Cheers for Kennedy, Released."
116. *New York Tribune*, "Dr. Kennedy Out on Bail."
117. *National Police Gazette*, "A Mysterious Suicide."
118. Ibid.

BIBLIOGRAPHY

GENERAL INFORMATION

Bayles, Richard, ed. *History of Richmond County, (Staten Island), New York from Its Discovery to the Present Time*. New York: L.E. Preston and Company, 1887.

Beers, F.W. "Atlas of Staten Island, Richmond County, New York." 1874.

Beers, J.B. "Atlas of Staten Island, Richmond County, New York." 1887.

Colton, G.W., and C.B. Colton. "Map of Staten Island, Richmond County, State of New York." 1896.

Dripps, Matthew. "Map of Staten Island, (Richmond County), N.Y." 1872.

Judson, Selden C. *Illustrated Sketchbook of Staten Island, New York, Its Industries and Commerce*. New York: S.C. Judson, 1886.

Leng, Charles W., and William T. Davis. *Staten Island and Its People*. Vols. 1–5. New York: Lewis Historical Publishing, 1930–33.

Morris, Ira K. *Morris' Memorial History of Staten Island, Volume 1*. New York: Memorial Publishing Company, 1898.

———. *Morris' Memorial History of Staten Island, Volume 2*. New York: self-published, 1900.

Robinson, E. "Atlas of the Borough of Richmond." 1907.

Scott, Kenneth. "A Murder on Staten Island in 1744." *Staten Island Historian* (January–March 1953).

Wallings, H.F. "Map of the City of New-York and Its Environs." 1860.

CHAPTER 1: FASCINATING DISCLOSURES

American Union. March 20, 1860.
Belmont Chronicle. "The Brennan [*sic*] Mystery." May 3, 1860.
Brooklyn Eagle. "The Box Mystery Explained." April 7, 1859.
Buffalo Courier and Republic. July 23, 1862.
Daily National Republican. "The Brannan Divorce Case." May 22, 1863.
Daily Union and American. September 5, 1858.
Evening Express. "The Brannon Divorce Case." May 22, 1863.
———. "The Case of Mrs. Brannan." August 1858.
———. "Local Intelligence." February 1859.
———. March 1860.
———. "The Staten Island Mystery—Again." September 3, 1858.
Evening Post. "The Massachusetts Regiments in the Fights." July 5, 1862.
Evening Star. "The Massachusetts Legislature." January 22, 1862.
———. April 7, 1859.
Nashville Union and American. "The Brannan Mystery." March 4, 1859.
New York Herald. "City Intelligence." August 13, 1858.
———. "$500 Reward." August 13, 1858.
———. "Military Affairs in New York." August 19, 1861.
———. "$200 Reward." July 28, 1858.
New York Times. "Gen. John M. Brannan." December 17, 1892.
Rhinebeck Gazette. "The Brannan Divorce Case." June 2, 1863.
Rochester Daily Union and Advertiser. "The Brannan Divorce Case." March 3, 1862.
Troy Daily Times. April 25, 1860.

CHAPTER 2: THE REFUSAL

Albany Argus. "Death of a Murderer." September 1848.
New York Herald. "Suicide by Starvation." September 19, 1848.
———. "A Wife Murdered by Her Husband." September 1848.
New York Tribune. "Inquest on Slaight." September 1848.
———. "Murder." September 11, 1848.
———. "The Murderer Caught." September 12, 1848.

CHAPTER 3: KILLED BY A SWORD CANE

Brooklyn Eagle. "Flaccomio Not Positively Identified." April 11, 1884.
———. "He Was Killed in a Duel." July 25, 1886.
———. "An Interesting Murder Case." April 8, 1884.
———. "Murder." April 7, 1884.
New York Times. "Antonio Flaccomio Discharged." April 13, 1884.
———. "Carmilio Farach's Death." April 8, 1884.
———. "Fatally Stabbed." October 15, 1888.
———. "Was It a Duel?" July 26, 1886.
Sun. "Killed with a Sword Cane." April 7, 1884.
———. "Was It a Life for a Life?" October 16, 1888.
World. "It Is 'The Mafia' Now." October 22, 1888.
———. "Still a Mystery." October 16, 1888.

CHAPTER 4: "YOU'LL EXPOSE ME; I KNOW YOU WILL!"

Bogert, Dr. *Sailors' Snug Harbor Record of Officers & Inmates, 1833–1872.* From the Archives of the Noble Maritime Collection.
Evening Express. "Staten Island." February 1863.
New York Times. "Murder and Suicide on Staten Island." February 1, 1863.
Shepherd, Barnett. *Sailors' Snug Harbor, 1801–1976.* New York: Furthermore Press, 1995.
Stoutenburgh, Henry Augustus. "Quinn, Robert." In *History of the Dutch Congregation of Oyster Bay, Queens County.* New York: Knickerbocker Press, 1906.

CHAPTER 5: A KNIFE IN THE TEMPLE

Daily Graphic. "The Killing of Edward Drury." October 12, 1885.
New York Herald. "Held for Trial." October 14, 1885.
———. "A Knife in the Temple." October 12, 1885.

New York Times. "City and Suburban News." November 6, 1885.
———. "Death After a Brawl." October 12, 1885.
———. "A Pardon Asked for Barbour." April 16, 1886.
Richmond County Gazette. October 24, 1885.
Syracuse Daily Standard. "The Governor Pardons a Murderer." September 8, 1886.
World. "Held for Trial for Murder." October 14, 1885.

CHAPTER 6: DUELING: WITH KEEN-EDGED SPADES

Daily Palladium. "Like Oneida Community." March 27, 1901.
Evening Post. "The Straight-Edge People's Plan." March 27, 1901.
Evening Telegram. Advertisement. August 21, 1901.
New York Press. "Old Man Drops Dead at Murder Trial." July 23, 1902.
———. "Sing Sing for Lay Preacher." July 24, 1902.
New York Times. "Straight Edgers' Society." March 25, 1901.
Sun. "Apply the Golden Rule." March 25, 1901.
———. "Business Troubles." January 22, 1919.
———. "Straight Edge Life Hard." June 1, 1901.
———. "The Straight Edge People." August 4, 1901.
———. "The Straight Edge 16." March 28, 1901.
———. "Was Straight Edger; in Jail." April 14, 1902.
———. "Wilbur F. Copeland." August 3, 1943.
———. "Young Woman Found Drowned." July 26, 1902.
World. "Fell Dead at Minister's Murder Trial." July 22, 1902.
———. "Minister Guilty of Manslaughter." July 23, 1902.

CHAPTER 7: DANCER WITH A WOODEN LEG

Auburn Citizen. "Two Girls Murdered in Gotham." April 6, 1923.
Brooklyn Daily Eagle. "Two Arraigned in Staten Island Double Murder." April 7, 1923.
———. "2 Girls Found Slain, Brutally Cut Bodies Hurled Out of Auto." April 6, 1923.

Brooklyn Standard Union. "S.I. Murder Victim Is Finally Buried." April 11, 1923.
———. "Startling Turn Expected in Dual Slasher Murder." April 7, 1923.
———. "Wrong Identification of One Victim Adds to Mystery of Murders." April 8, 1923.
Daily Argus. "Detectives at Cortland Inquiry About Former Husband of Mrs. Blandino." April 16, 1923.
———. "Two Slain Women Tossed From Auto on Staten Island Road." April 6, 1923.
Daily Sentinel. "Blandino Woman Friend of Ponzi." April 10, 1923.
Evening Telegram. "Believe Auto Used in Dual Slaying Is Found." April 7, 1923.
———. "Husband Claims Slain Wife's Body." April 13, 1923.
———. "2 Men Held on $20,000 Each in Dual Slaying." April 9, 1923.
New York Times. "Boy Finds Body of Murdered Man." December 5, 1923.
———. "Murder Witness Freed." April 11, 1923.
———. "Seek First Husband in Double Murder." April 9, 1923.
———. "Staten Island Clue to Girl Slayers." April 10, 1923.
———. "Three Men Sought for Slaying Women." April 8, 1923.
———. "Two Women Slain; Suspect Gang Plot." April 27, 1923.
Reycraft, Jack. "1923—Two Bodies in Dongan Hills." *Staten Island Advance*, August 27, 1951.
Rome Daily Sentinel. "Murdered Girls Put up Desperate Fight to Save Their Lives." April 7, 1923.
Staten Island Advance. "Bodies of Two Girls with Throats Cut Found by Milkman on Lonely Road." April 6, 1923.
Union-Sun and Journal. "Two Women Slain in a Lonely Spot on Staten Island." April 6, 1923.
Utica Observer-Dispatch. "Di Pasquale Sought by Police Probing Murder of Women." April 10, 1923.
———. "Girl Last Home in December Urged to Stay." April 6, 1923.
———. "Girl's Father Declares Black Hand Lies Back of Daughter's Murder." April 6, 1923.
———. "Never Happy But Always Smiling Was Elvira Salerno, Murdered." April 6, 1923.
———. "Other Murdered Girl Was Not from This City." April 8, 1923.
———. "Salerno Girl Had Divorced One Husband." April 6, 1923.
———. "Slain Girl in Custody Here Twice." April 6, 1923.

CHAPTER 8: A RUM RAID GONE AWRY

Brooklyn Eagle. "Arrest 5 in Whisky Deal as Dying Man Gives Names." March 9, 1922.

———. "Indict 2 Brooklyn Men for Conspiracy in Bootleg Murder." March 14, 1922.

———. "Start Murder Trial for Connor's Death." April 17, 1922.

Brooklyn Standard Union. "Jury Convicts Collins of Watchman's Murder." April 22, 1922.

Evening Telegram. "To Bare Rum Ring at Murder Trail." April 17, 1922.

———. "Four Indicted in Bootleg Murder." March 11, 1922.

———. "Least Coveted Title." November 7, 1922.

Evening World. "First of 4 Trials Begun for Murder in Whiskey Raid." April 17, 1922.

———. "Gunmen Planned to Kill Boy with Them in Rum Raid." April 26, 1922.

———. "Jurors 'Get Air' in Autos to be Fit for Murder Trial." April 19, 1922.

———. "New Trial for Man in Prison Death House." December 20, 1922.

———. "Six Men Indicted, Four for Murder, in Bootleg Slaying." March 11, 1922.

New York Call. "High Brow Death House Champ." November 6, 1922.

New York Times. "Death House to Freedom." June 15, 1923.

———. "Nine Face Court Today." April 17, 1922.

New York Tribune. "Betray Slayers or Risk Death, Court Tells Man." April 25, 1922.

CHAPTER 9: PLACED IN JEOPARDY—NIGHTLY

Brooklyn Daily Eagle. "2 Men Slain Here in Sabbath Feuds; Body Found in Lot." October 25, 1920.

New York Times. "Identify Woman Slain in Thicket." October 24, 1920.

———. "Witness Gives Clue to Woman's Murder." March 17, 1921.

New York Tribune. "Slain Woman Is Identified by Husband." October 24, 1920.

Reycraft, Jack. "1920—West Brighton Strangling." *Staten Island Advance*, October 5, 1951.

Standard Union. "Husband Identifies Victim of Strangler." October 24, 1920.

CHAPTER 10: A FORMER CABARET BEAUTY AND HER DASHING YOUNG SERGEANT

Brooklyn Daily Eagle. "First Lunacy Trial Is Held Before U.S. Court Here." March 28, 1932.

New York Evening Post. "Army Man Hunted in Killing of Wife." January 4, 1932.

New York Sun. "Clew to Army Killing." January 5, 1932.

———. "Hunt Army Man as Wife Slayer." January 4, 1932.

New York Times. "Army Man Seized for Wife's Murder." March 6, 1932.

———. "Army Sergeant Faces Civil Trial in Murder." March 7, 1932.

———. "Clue Speeds Murder Hunt." January 7, 1932.

———. "Find Soldier's Wife Shot Dead in Home." January 4, 1932.

———. "New Clue in Killing of Sergeant's Wife." January 6, 1932.

———. "Soldier Killer Held Insane." January 7, 1932.

Rochester Democrat and Chronicle. "Finds Indictment in Elsie Smith Slaying." January 5, 1932.

Sullivan, Gerard. "Who Killed These 8 Women?" *Staten Island Advance*, January 9, 1932.

Syracuse Journal. "Sergeant Who Slew Wife Adjudged Insane." March 29, 1932.

CHAPTER 11: UNANSWERED FOR EIGHTY-THREE YEARS

Brooklyn Daily Eagle. "Slayer's Victim on S.I. Identified as Missing Nurse." June 8, 1931.

Mogelever, Bernard. "Our Unsolved Murders: Body Found in Woods." *Staten Island Advance*, September 26, 1965.

New York Times. "Nurse Found Slain in Richmond Woods." June 8, 1931.

————. "Query Coast Guards in Death of Nurse, 19." June 9, 1931.
Standard Union. "Missing Girl's Body Found on Staten Island." June 8, 1931.

CHAPTER 12: A CASE OF MURDER—A MOST BRUTAL ONE

Brooklyn Eagle. "Dr. Kennedy Released on a Bond of $10,000." June 18, 1901.
————. "Dr. Kennedy Sentenced." March 31, 1899.
————. "Found Dead in a Hotel." August 16, 1898.
————. "Kennedy Held for Murder." August 17, 1898.
————. "Kennedy's Trial Begun." February 4, 1901.
————. "Kennedy to be Tried Again." February 25, 1901.
————. "Mrs. Logue on the Stand." March 25, 1899.
Buffalo Evening Express. "Kennedy Jury Fails to Reach an Agreement." June 17, 1901.
Evening Post. "The Grand Hotel Murder." August 17, 1898.
Evening Press. "On the Tip of the Tongue." September 1, 1898.
Evening Telegram. "Kennedy Not Held by Coroner's Jury." August 30, 1898.
National Police Gazette. "A Mysterious Suicide." April 1, 1893.
New York Herald. "Murder Ends Her Hotel Romance." August 17, 1898.
New York Times. "The Case of Dr. Kennedy." August 31, 1898.
————. "The Grand Hotel Murder." August 18, 1898.
————. "Kennedy Sentenced to Die." April 1, 1899.
————. "Reynolds Murder Case." August 20, 1898.
————. "Woman Murdered in Hotel." August 17, 1898.
New York Tribune. "Counsel for Kennedy." December 21, 1899.
————. "Court Releases the Heathmeres." May 16, 1901.
————. "Dr. Kennedy Out on Bail." June 19, 1901.
————. "Experts Begin Their Innings." May 24, 1901.
————. "Good Day for Kennedy." May 17, 1901.
————. "Kennedy on Trial Again." May 7, 1901.
————. "Kennedy's Defense Alibi." March 30, 1899.
————. "Kennedy Trial Fairly Begun." February 8, 1901.
————. "Molineux Is Cheerful." February 18, 1900.
————. "New Trial for Kennedy." November 21, 1900.
————. "Says Kennedy Was a Tool." November 22, 1900.

Prominent Men of Staten Island. New York: A.Y. Hubell, 1893.

Sun. "Cheers for Kennedy, Released." June 19, 1901.

———. "Did Kennedy Murder Her?" August 18, 1898.

———. "Dolly Reynolds's Murder." March 30 1899.

———. "The Dolly Reynolds Murder. March 29, 1899.

———. "Kennedy Jury Completed." May 15, 1901.

———. "Kennedy Jury Is Split." June 16, 1901.

———. "Kennedy Witness Fined." February 21, 1901.

———. "Mendham Figures Again." June 12, 1901.

———. "Mother and Child Crazy?" May 12, 1901.

———. "Mysterious Heathmeres." May 13, 1901.

———. "No Retrial for Kennedy." November 27, 1901.

———. "Says He Killed Dolly Reynolds." May 6, 1899.

———. "Sure Kennedy Killed Her." August 21, 1898.

———. "Woman Testifies for Kennedy." June 8, 1901.

World. "Bludgeon Evidence for Dr. Kennedy." February 13, 1901.

———. "Broker Mendham to Tell of Dolly Reynolds's Life." May 15, 1901.

———. "Broker Mendham Tells of Dolly Reynolds's Life." May 16, 1901.

———. "Claims Most of $100,000." December 27, 1901.

———. "Delay in the Kennedy Case." June 17, 1901.

———. "Dr. Kennedy Fiercely Arraigned, Now Awaits Judge's Last Word." June 14, 1901.

———. "Eight to Four for Kennedy." June 15, 1901.

———. "Four Witnesses Saw Kennedy on Fatal Day." February 18, 1901.

———. "'I Am Innocent' Says Dr. Kennedy." February 15, 1901.

———. "Kennedy Chooses Men to Decide His Fate." February 6, 1901.

———. "Kennedy Jury Disagrees." February 22, 1901.

———. "Kennedy Is Victim of Plot." June 13, 1901.

———. "Kennedy's Judge Gets Anonymous Letters." February 19, 1901.

———. "Kennedy's Life Staked on Alibi Now Building." February 19, 1901.

———. "The Lead Pipe May Save Dr. Kennedy." October 10, 1900.

———. "Maurice Mendham Dead; Broadway Recalls His Career." November 8, 1912.

———. "May Indict Melville." February 13, 1901.

———. "Says Kennedy's the Man." February 11, 1901.

———. "Who Murdered Dolly Reynolds and Why?" August 17, 1898.

———. "Will Testify on Handwriting." May 22, 1901.

Yonkers Statesman. "To Marry Her Guardian." February 26, 1912.

ABOUT THE AUTHOR

Patricia M. Salmon retired as curator of history from the Staten Island Museum in 2012. A Staten Island resident for almost fifty years, she was a naturalist/historian at Clay Pit Ponds State Park Preserve in that borough for eight years. Ms. Salmon has authored the books *Realms of History: The Cemeteries of Staten Island*, *The Staten Island Ferry: A History* and *Murder & Mayhem on Staten Island*. A board member of the Tottenville Historical Society, she is an adjunct professor at Wagner College in Staten Island and a guest contributor to the "Memories" column of the *Staten Island Advance*.

Patricia M. Salmon with the late historian Hugh Powell, 2013. *Photograph by Barbara Hemedinger.*